"Why We Drop Out"

"Why We Drop Out"

Understanding and Disrupting Student Pathways to Leaving School

Deborah L. Feldman
Antony T. Smith
Barbara L. Waxman

Foreword by Camille Farrington

TEACHERS COLLEGE PRESS

TEACHERS COLLEGE | COLUMBIA UNIVERSITY

NEW YORK AND LONDON

Published by Teachers College Press, 1234 Amsterdam Avenue, New York, NY 10027

Copyright © 2017 by Teachers College, Columbia University

Cover photo by Saša Prudkov, Dreamstime.

Library of Congress Cataloging-in-Publication Data is available at loc.gov

ISBN 978-0-8077-5862-5 (paper)
ISBN 978-0-8077-7616-2 (ebook)

Printed on acid-free paper
Manufactured in the United States of America

24 23 22 21 20 19 18   8 7 6 5 4 3 2

Contents

Foreword

Around 2005, I went to listen to Gary Orfield give a lecture at the Chicago Public Library. I had returned to graduate school to get my PhD after 15 years teaching high school, and I was obsessed with studying the trajectories of academic failure. Professor Orfield had just edited a great volume called *Dropouts in America: Confronting the Graduation Rate Crisis* that pulled together the best of what was known on that topic. Drawing from his work as director of the Civil Rights Project at Harvard, he shared stories and statistics about young people—mostly low-income and African American or Latino youth—who dropped out or were pushed out of high school without a diploma, as well as the long-term social and economic consequences for their lives and their communities. After his lecture, I went up to talk with him. I shared that, as a teacher, I had seen students struggle and drop out of school while other very similar students defied the odds and graduated. "In your experience," I asked, "what makes the difference between the kids who make it and the kids who drop out?" He thought for a minute and said, "The ones who make it, they all have some adult who, at some point, grabs onto them and pulls them over the line."

I was reminded of Professor Orfield's words as I read this compelling new book by Deborah Feldman, Antony Smith, and Barbara Waxman. Drawing from oral histories of youth in western Washington State who had left school without a diploma, the authors illuminate very human stories behind the dropout statistics. They reveal a picture of young people who were floundering around in plain view, looking for a lifeline, but who didn't seem to have anybody there to effectively reach out and grab onto them.

In some ways, the stories we find here are very familiar: academic difficulties, troubles at home, conflicts with teachers, progressive disengagement from school. What this book adds is a longer-term view and a broader narrative, capturing memories of early (and almost wholly enjoyable) schooling experiences in elementary and middle school, and paying attention to the critical importance of peer relationships and conflicts in shaping young people's paths through and out of school. The authors not only provide a humanizing view into the lives of these youth; they also offer concrete, practical suggestions for how teachers and school leaders might provide critical supports for vulnerable young people who otherwise might make the very regrettable decision to drop out of high school.

This book comes at a time when there is much evidence available to support improvements in high school instruction. Advances in the fields of neuroscience and psychology make it clear that learning is as much a psychosocial process as it is a cognitive one. Put simply, what a young person feels and believes influences what he or she can learn. The youth we meet in this book struggle to engage in schools that fundamentally fail to meet their psychosocial needs as adolescents. The very design of their high schools breeds alienation and undermines deep learning—days chopped into 45-minute blocks of rotating subject matter, teachers with too many students to provide individual help, grading systems that penalize struggling students for not getting things right the first time, and instructional practices that leave students feeling exposed and humiliated in front of their peers. These contextual factors systematically undermine student mindsets that are critical to academic performance: feelings of belonging, relevance, self-efficacy, and growth mindset.

In the stories captured here, school often takes on the specter of a fast-moving train that students are forever try to catch but never can. As they reflect back on their high school experience, the young people describe themselves as being "off track," "slow," and, almost inevitably, "too far behind" to pass. Their voices are haunting as they reflect upon the myriad challenges that caused them to withdraw from school short of reaching the academic goals they had set for themselves. An important contribution of this book is its compelling reminder to take time to ask young people for their stories, and to listen attentively to their answers. We make a powerful move when we shift from focusing on the "what" of student behavior—what they are or are not doing that is undermining their success—to asking them to help us understand the "why" behind that behavior, and what we might do to be of help.

While the authors provide a sobering account of the realities that lead young people to drop out, embedded in these pages is also clear evidence of the transformative power of teachers and school administrators to keep students in school. Every educator will recognize in these stories the daily opportunities that adults have to reach out and grab onto kids who are desperate for a hand and just need someone to pull them over that line.

—Camille A. Farrington, PhD
Author, *Failing at School: Lessons for Redesigning Urban High Schools* (2014)
Chicago, Illinois

Acknowledgments

First, we wish to thank the many youths who agreed to share with us their personal and often quite painful stories about leaving school. Their candid voices are at the heart of this book. In addition, we are grateful to the many partnering agencies and individuals that gave us advice, brought us into contact with these youths, and supported the recruitment and interviewing process. Finally, we wish to acknowledge critical funding support this project received from the Washington State Partnership Council on Juvenile Justice, the Washington Educational Research Association, and the Goodlad Institute for Educational Renewal at the University of Washington Bothell.

Introduction

People think they know who we are. . . . They think dropouts
are all the same, but we're not! We leave school for all different
reasons; sometimes we leave because we just have to.
—Magdalena, age 18, who left school at 17 to work and to care
for a child

This book brings fresh perspective to a well-documented problem: the
large number of students across the country who leave school prema-
turely. It follows the stories of young people with differing interests and
abilities, representing diverse communities and family backgrounds,
who share one important characteristic that transcends their differences:
They all made the life-altering decision to quit school before graduating.
How did they arrive at this decision? What experiences shaped their
perceptions of themselves as students? Could their schools have done
anything along the way to divert them from their pathways to dropping out?

LISTENING TO YOUTH PERSPECTIVES

In order to explore the "why" of dropping out and the mechanisms
behind it, we developed the Washington Student Oral Histories Project,
a university–community collaboration involving an interdisciplinary
team of researchers. We wanted to bring something new to the conversation about dropping out by investigating the phenomenon from the
perspectives of young people themselves. While research has examined
the dropout issue, youth perspectives have been largely absent from
these investigations. Studies examining student opinion have relied
primarily on focus groups and structured interviews (see Bridgeland,
Dilulio, & Morison, 2006, for example). Although these methods have
revealed important aspects of the dropping out experience, they do not

1

allow for in-depth exploration, reflection, or historical perspective-taking on the part of young people.

During the 2012–2013 school year, our interview team gathered oral histories from a racially, ethnically, and geographically diverse group of 53 young people in western Washington State who were between the ages of 16 and 22 and previously had dropped out of school. Youths of color who self-identified as Asian, African American, Hispanic, Native American, or "other" constituted 57% of this study group. At the time of the interview, 45% of the group were living in an urban setting, while the remainder came from suburban or rural settings.

Determining who was actually a "dropout" and who was merely "truant" was not always easy. There is no standard definition of how long a student needs to be out of school to be considered "dropped out." Moreover, school enrollment records are often incomplete and out of date (Tyler & Lofstrom, 2009). For this study, we considered anyone who elected to stay completely out of school for 1 month or more to have "dropped out." Being truant for a month virtually ensured that students would be too far behind to catch up and would fail their classes for either the semester or the year. Using a conversational approach and semistructured interview protocol, our research team interviewed individual youths, prompting them to share their experiences from early years in school through the point at which they dropped out. The stories of six selected young people, three female and three male, are included in this book. Further details on study participants and methodology are provided in the Appendix.

The stories shared by youth participants in our study belie stereotypes of "dropouts" as delinquents, often from dysfunctional families, who don't care about school or learning. Listening to youths' stories allows us to move past these stereotypes, providing an opportunity to better understand the spectrum of challenges these vulnerable young people have faced and, in some instances, overcome. These stories reveal, for example, that the overwhelming majority of interviewed youths experienced academic challenges that undermined their faith in themselves as learners, leading to a debilitating sense of helplessness and hopelessness, academic failure, and, ultimately, a rejection of school. For many, their academic difficulties preceded and precipitated truancy (as well as other delinquent behaviors)—not the reverse. In addition, this group faced a range of personal challenges, including economic and housing instability, homelessness, health issues, and family dysfunction. Disruptive forces in their personal lives, in combination with school difficulties, created a perfect storm that overwhelmed these vulnerable youths, propelling them along a pathway to dropping out.

The findings of our study both confirm and expand upon previous research linking aspects of school learning contexts (e.g., interactions with teachers and peers, instructional methods and curricula, school climate, and discipline policies) to student attitudes and outcomes, including dropping out (Bridgeland et al., 2006; Farrington, 2014; Rumberger, 2011). Through youths' stories we come to understand the dropping out process with greater clarity and nuance, especially in terms of specific school factors that can influence this process. Not only are these stories about failure and loss; they also incorporate positive experiences that motivated youths, sometimes keeping them in school for extended periods and persuading them to return to and stay in school after initially dropping out. Their stories suggest that to be successful in diverting students from negative pathways, schools need to move well beyond early warning systems, truancy proceedings, and other more traditional approaches to preventing dropouts.

SCHOOL FACTORS CONNECTED TO DROPPING OUT: KEY THEMES

Across the diverse experiences and backgrounds of youth interviewees, several dominant themes emerged from their stories, providing insights into the complex nature of the dropping out process and how schools might intervene to prevent or reverse it. Below we present three overarching ideas derived from our analysis of youths' stories and discuss implications for the development of effective dropout prevention programs.

Complex Intertwined Factors

The factors that propel students toward dropping out are both complex and deeply intertwined. Youth participants talked to us at length about their educational experiences, how they perceived and reacted to those experiences, and how their thinking, emotions, and behavior related to school evolved over time. In almost all instances, no single factor explained how an individual came to drop out. Rather, a complex web of school and nonschool factors propelled them toward skipping school, course failure, and, ultimately, dropping out.

Most youth interviewees, for example, faced learning challenges at various points in their educational journey that unsettled them and led them to doubt their capabilities. ("I'll never be able to do this work.") In addition, many admitted that they did not really understand the importance of good study habits ("I never turned in homework.") and did not apply themselves when work became difficult. As we will learn, these factors mutually reinforced one another over time, leading to ever-increasing academic problems that eventually spiraled out of control and were seemingly impervious to intervention.

In addition to academic problems, at least half of our youth participants admitted to behavioral issues that led to disciplinary actions, which, in turn, increased their ambivalence toward school. Sometimes these issues appeared to stem from mental health challenges (e.g., impulsive behavior due to attention deficit disorder), unstable or conflict-filled homes, or personal trauma. In other cases, interviewees connected their negative behavior to the school environment itself—unmet learning needs, negative interactions with school personnel, or hostile peers. A majority of interviewees also revealed serious personal or family-related problems that diverted their energy and focus away from school.

An effective dropout prevention program needs to respond to the multiplicity and complexity of factors leading to students' detachment from school. Such a program expands its focus beyond student behavior, delving into the attitudes, experiences, and perceptions that drive student behaviors. Thus, a first step in creating a comprehensive program aimed at addressing this complexity of intertwined factors is listening to struggling students in order to understand their perspectives on the challenges that they face.

Relationships and a Sense of Belonging

For all students, but especially for struggling students, relationships and a sense of belonging are at the heart of the learning enterprise. Contrary to what many people might assume about dropouts, the overwhelming majority of the young people we interviewed started their school careers on a positive note. A major reason they gave for their fond memories of their elementary years was the caring, supportive personal relationships they experienced with teachers. Once they entered middle school, these relationships seemed to disappear. Youths' generally negative perceptions of secondary teachers (whether accurate or not) deeply affected their enjoyment of school, dampened their participation in class, reduced their willingness to approach teachers for help, and decreased their motivation to persevere.

A related issue for struggling students entering middle school was the sudden loss of community. The anchors to community they relied on in elementary school—a caring teacher who provided both emotional and academic support, a small and largely unchanging class, a set cohort of peers—were largely absent in the middle school context. Youth interviewees often struggled to find ways of belonging in a new, much larger school community. Many felt educationally abandoned and unable to fully participate in their classes, feeding a destructive narrative of "I don't fit in here."

Discipline practices unwittingly served to reinforce this narrative by chastising and punishing students for their observed behavior without taking into account the context surrounding that behavior or providing ways for youths to redeem themselves. Punishments sometimes reduced unacceptable behaviors in the short term, but were ultimately counterproductive, increasing students' sense of resentment, alienation from the community, and desire to avoid school.

For these reasons, effective dropout prevention must involve schoolwide efforts to build community and enhance teacher–student relationships at every grade level. Such efforts are naturally more difficult in the larger, more complex institutional settings of most secondary schools. Figuring out how to sustain positive relationships and create new connections to community for all students is a central challenge for secondary schools committed to preventing dropouts. A related challenge is to create discipline programs that hold students accountable while also acknowledging their needs and perspectives, and teaching them the social-emotional skills needed to manage feelings and social situations.

Disengaging Instructional Practices

Traditional instructional practices are mismatched to struggling students' needs. Most interviewees remembered being excited about learning when they were little, and largely bored and uninterested in their classes when they were older. Traditional teaching methods at the secondary level typically failed to spark their interest and motivate them to learn, especially when they doubted their capabilities as learners, were afraid of failing, and could not see the relevance of class content to their own lives. Other common practices around testing and grading further discouraged already discouraged learners. A comprehensive dropout prevention program, therefore, needs to review pedagogical practices, especially at the secondary level, and replace those practices that demonstrably do not serve the interests of all students with more interactive and engaging practices.

This book explores not only ways in which young people fail school, but also how school, in turn, fails them. Youths' stories suggest that our educational institutions need to reflect deeply on their own role in the dropping out process and to alter policies and practices that are inadvertently harmful to vulnerable young people.

ORGANIZATION OF THE BOOK

We open the first chapter with background on the scope of the dropping out problem and its broader significance to society. Chapter 1 also describes common patterns of behavior related to dropping out that emerged from youths' narratives. These patterns provide a framework for understanding how the dropout process typically progresses over time and how the process might vary, depending on an individual youth's circumstances.

Chapters 2, 3, and 4 describe school experiences and trace the dropping out process as it unfolds in elementary, middle, and high school. In these chapters we explore academic challenges, learning environments, and social factors in school, paying special attention to how school experiences may encourage truant behavior and factor into the dropping out process.

The next two chapters are thematically organized: Chapter 5 explores nonschool factors influencing the dropout process, including health, family, and social issues. We consider ways these factors, such as social skipping, alcohol and drug use, and family instability, impact the process of dropping out of school. Chapter 6 focuses on youths' experiences exiting school and their perceptions of the ultimate "tipping points" they believed led them to quit school. We examine the different kinds of tipping points youth participants identified, including bullying, expulsion, pregnancy, and homelessness, and show which have been well-documented in the research and which add new facets to the complex picture of leaving school permanently.

Following Chapters 3, 4, and 5, we have included full-length youth narratives as stand-alone inter-chapters. These narratives offer more detailed personal accounts of each of six young people who, collectively, represent important themes and experiences from the larger sample of young people interviewed. The full-length narratives provide context for the excerpted quotes from these six individuals that appear throughout the book, preserving the arc of their educational histories from their earliest school years to the present day. The narratives are aimed at readers interested in further exploring these youths' perspectives at different stages of their school experience.

The final chapter moves from identifying causal factors to seeking practical solutions. It connects what has been learned to pragmatic steps that schools can take to encourage and support struggling students. While we recognize that schools cannot address all the vulnerabilities that young people bring to classroom settings, there is still much that schools can accomplish by identifying and replacing counterproductive policies and practices with ones more supportive of at-risk youth. In this last chapter, we identify specific strategies that are likely to support vulnerable students and divert them from common pathways to dropping out.

CHAPTER 1

Pathways to Dropping Out

I didn't wanna drop out. I had a lot of extenuating circumstances that made it difficult for me to graduate, and eventually, it was just too much. I had to stop. —Callie

This chapter highlights major patterns that emerged from our interviews with dozens of young people about their pathways to dropping out—patterns we will explore throughout the book. To illustrate our research-based findings, we incorporate excerpts from the narratives of six representative youths we interviewed (whose full-length narratives are provided as inter-chapters). Before delving into these key ideas about the dropping out process, we begin with some context for understanding the scope of the problem.

THE PROBLEM (WHY SHOULD WE CARE ABOUT THIS?)

In the United States, one of the most advanced postindustrial nations in the world, the scope of the dropout problem is surprising. Although high school graduation rates have ticked up several percentage points in recent years, about half a million high school students still drop out of school annually (Stetser & Stillwell, 2014). Official statistics place the 2014 national on-time graduation rate at 82% for all students (Snyder, de Brey, & Dillow, 2016). However, some experts have argued that these statistics are misleading (Kamenetz et al., 2015). Investigative reporting has uncovered multiple "quick fix" strategies being used by districts across the country to boost graduation rates, including routinely misreporting "dropouts" as "transfers" out of the district (Turner, 2015). While graduation rates may have risen, evidence suggests that student skill levels have not; many diploma holders remain woefully unprepared for college and career (Rich, 2015).[1]

In addition, the overall graduation rate masks the seriousness of this problem for various student subpopulations. For example, at the national level, White and Asian students do comparatively well; they have on-time graduation rates of 87% and 89%, respectively. By contrast, the on-time high school completion rate for African American and Native American students hovers around 72% and 70%, respectively; for Hispanic students the rate is 76%. State-level graduation rates reveal greater disparities: In a number of states, more than one third of students of color fail to graduate on time (Snyder et al., 2016).

Analysis of graduation rates by other demographic characteristics also reveals striking differences in educational attainment among different groups. As shown in Figure 1.1, students from low-income families graduate at a substantially lower rate (75%) than their more advantaged peers (89%). For students with disabilities, on-time graduation rates are especially dismal, with only 63% graduating in 4 years (Civic Enterprises & Everyone Graduates Center, 2016).[2]

Examining annual *dropout events* (as opposed to graduation rates) further reveals the deep connection between family economic status and educational attainment: Students whose family income falls in the lowest quartile drop out at a rate four times higher than students in the upper quartile (Snyder et al., 2016). Of those who drop out, some find their way back to school and are able to earn a diploma by age 21 (the cutoff age for educational services used in many public school districts). But many of these early school-leavers do not return right away, or they return only to drop out again. They flounder, sometimes for years, lacking meaningful connections to school and struggling to find stable or rewarding work, as employment trends in the 21st century have dramatically narrowed their options.

Figure 1.1. National Graduation Rates by Income, Disability

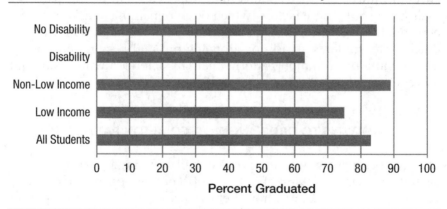

Source: Civic Enterprises & Everyone Graduates Center (2016).

Fewer and fewer nongraduates are able to participate successfully in the workforce, and those who do participate are largely consigned to jobs offering below-poverty wages (Swanson, 2009). These broad trends portend ever-increasing income disparities among racial, geographic, and economic subpopulations, based in large measure on their varying graduation rates. Those who graduate from high school, but obtain no further training or education, have an exceedingly difficult time finding sufficient work to attain a livable wage. Those who fail to graduate often cannot manage even to secure a stable source of income.

School systems around the country increasingly have been deploying predictive "early warning systems" to identify youth at risk for dropping out. Typically, these systems use readily available student data on attendance, grades, and behavior to flag high-risk students for academic supports or other interventions.[3] These early warning systems are based on research confirming the connection between certain observable student behaviors and later academic outcomes (Rumberger & Lim, 2008). We know, for instance, that multiple absences and course failure in core 8th-grade subjects are highly predictive of failure and dropping out in high school. However, the predictive models upon which early warning systems are based tell us only *what* behavior to look for, not *why* the behavior is occurring in the first place or what we should do about it.

The purpose of this book is to explore the "why" of it all, in the belief that asking why is an essential step toward better prevention as well as intervention. Why, for example, are certain middle school students failing 8th-grade math or missing up to 15 days of school in a single semester? Youths' stories provide a window into the individual experiences, attitudes, and perceptions that propelled them onto a pathway to dropping out. These factors (which often remain hidden from school personnel) can provide insights into how schools might identify, in a timely way, students at risk for dropping out and respond effectively. Determining the common patterns that characterize the dropping out process is an important first step in addressing the "why."

PATHWAYS TO DROPPING OUT: COMMON PATTERNS

Each young person we interviewed had a unique backstory connected to decisionmaking about school. Looking across their widely varying personal accounts, however, we discovered that youth participants tended to follow some common patterns of behavior related to dropping out—patterns previously hinted at (Rumberger, 2011) but not fully described in the literature. We begin with a description of distinct phases in the dropping out process that emerged from youths' narratives, followed by several other patterns of behavior; at the end of the chapter we discuss the implications of these patterns for intervening with youth.

Four Phases of Dropping Out

For the youths in our study, the dropping out process consisted of four distinct, but often overlapping, phases (Figure 1.2), beginning with *initial disengagement* from school and/or from learning. Subsequent phases included an *early skipping* phase, *more serious truancy,* and, finally, *dropping out*. Below we describe youth characteristics and behaviors that are associated with each phase.

Phase 1: Initial Disengagement. In this first phase, *disengagement* refers to a state of mind or emotional condition that reflects disinterest in or negative feelings toward learning or being in school. The term also refers to the observable behaviors associated with this state of mind/emotional condition. Our definition of disengagement borrows from Fredricks, Blumenfeld, and Paris (2004), who argue that the concept of school engagement should encompass three dimensions: cognitive, emotional, and behavioral. At this initial stage, many youths felt one or more of the following about school:

- I can't do this work. It's too hard.
- I'm too bored/distracted/unhappy/scared to focus in class.
- Other things besides school are more important to me right now.
- Why I should learn this? It doesn't seem relevant or important.

Figure 1.2. Phases in the Dropping Out Process

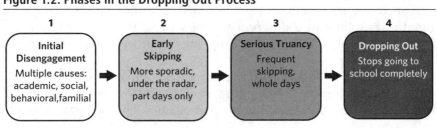

Before moving into the next phase, young people commonly manifested this initial sense of disengagement through overt academic behaviors, such as tuning out in class, ignoring homework, or failing tests.

Phase 2: Early Skipping. After developing negative sentiments about learning, and especially after beginning to perform poorly academically, participants often moved to a second phase characterized by experimental and sporadic skipping of individual classes. Frequently, youths chose to avoid those classes in which they felt the teacher did not care about them or in which they perceived they were not doing well, as typified by Xavier's explanation for skipping algebra:

> What classes did I start skipping? I think it was an English class . . . and then I think it was algebra class. I skipped algebra classes because . . . I can't really understand what that teacher is talking about. —Xavier

Phase 3: Serious Truancy. At some point, youth participants typically slid into a third phase of more serious truancy that was commonly the precursor to leaving school altogether. Youths in this phase skipped one or more classes regularly or missed whole days of school. Significant academic failure followed as they fell too far behind in their coursework to catch up, entering a downward spiral characterized by continual discouragement, low motivation, and a lack of academic progress. Trisha's attitude was representative of many others in our study:

> When 9th grade started, I was doing well. Then, a couple terms in I started getting F's and D's. Then, after that, I just didn't even want to try because I felt like it was too much work to get all my grades up. —Trisha

Phase 4: Dropping Out. In the final phase of the dropping out process, interviewees gave up on being students and ceased to attend school altogether for at least a month (our study definition of having "dropped out"). Sometimes they returned to school within a couple of months, enrolling in a different school setting. However, while these quick returns often delayed the dropping out process, they did not appear to halt it.

Our interview data suggest that certain definitive events and experiences propel already struggling students into this fourth and final phase of dropping out. We asked youth participants, *"Why do you think you decided to stop going to school?"* Most were able to identify pivotal events or "tipping points" they deemed critical to their final act of dropping out. Here are two very different kinds of explanations for leaving school:

> I had been skipping a lot. I came back on the last day of school only to have someone try to pick on me . . . and at that point I just knew I couldn't go back to that school. —Jack

> After skipping a lot, I started taking extra classes and working twice as hard. And then, at 17 I got pregnant. —Callie

Several other kinds of explanations figured prominently in interviewees' reflections about this final phase of dropping out; we'll discuss these tipping points further in Chapter 6.

Dropping Out Patterns

Thus far we have presented dropping out as a unidirectional process encompassing four phases and culminating in a final exit. However, youth participants also experienced variations within this general pattern, with many reaching a tipping point either quite quickly or quite slowly. In addition, some cycled through various phases more than once. We examine these underlying variations next.

Slow Faders. We considered young people to be "slow faders" if they appeared to stay in school 3 or more years after they first started avoiding school. These students, who constituted just over one third of the participant group, often displayed clear warning signs of disengagement well before high school. They typically commenced skipping behavior in middle school or early 9th grade and continued the behavior throughout high school, often not dropping out entirely until they were 18 or even 19 years old. Sometimes they improved their attendance and grades for a period, but then fell back into missing school, not completing work, and failing classes. Others have noted a similar up-and-down pattern of engagement during high school (Bridgeland et al., 2006), although we encountered this pattern at the middle school level as well.

At first glance, slow faders seem perplexing. What is the motivation for these young people to continue hanging on despite insufficient academic progress to graduate? They gave multiple reasons for persisting. For some, athletic activities or socializing with peers continued to draw them. For others, it was fear of being taken to truancy court and what parents would say or do, or the desire to comply with parental wishes. For still others, it was the inability to formulate an alternative plan for their future.

Xavier, identified as a slow fader, reported having school problems throughout his entire educational career, starting with behavioral issues in elementary school and progressing to academic and social problems in middle school. During high school, he routinely engaged in truancy, failed classes, and tangled with school personnel. Yet even after a drop-out period in his senior year, he continued with school. He credited his persistence, in part, to family members' influence. When asked what kept him coming to school despite disliking it for such a long time, Xavier responded:

> I didn't wanna be like everyone else in my family that didn't graduate. Or who got a GED or took online classes, or whatever. I didn't wanna end up like that. None of them really were happy with a GED. . . . If I went to school I would pretty much have it better than they had it growing up. —Xavier

Accelerated Leavers. About 30% of the young people we interviewed experienced dropping out on a compressed time schedule. These "accelerated leavers" moved rapidly from the early skipping phase to not attending at all; within a year after initial skipping they were gone. Accelerated leavers like Jack frequently had endured serious family situations and personal crises that overwhelmed them. Or, like Yolanda, the allure of gangs or street life quickly drew them away from school:

> In 9th grade I got introduced to teenage life, so I started going to the streets. I started smoking pot, doing drugs. I didn't care about school. I really didn't care anymore about anything. —Yolanda

Other factors contributing to a rapid departure from school included expulsion, homelessness, bullying, and pregnancy. Once accelerated leavers dropped out, they were more likely to stay out permanently or re-enroll only for short periods before dropping out again. They also tended to return to an alternative educational program only after a substantial hiatus, going for a general educational development (GED) credential rather than a diploma. It is important to note that while this certification is supposed to be equivalent to a diploma, with respect to long-term student outcomes it is not: GED certificate holders, on average, earn less and attend postsecondary education at substantially lower rates than diploma holders (Ewert, 2012).

Dropping In, Dropping Out. We found that some youth participants experienced the four phases of dropping out in a cyclical manner. Over time, they moved back and forth on a truancy–dropout continuum, attending for a period and then not attending. Moreover, more than one quarter of participants engaged in "serial" dropping out, that is, dropping out, re-enrolling, and then dropping out again—each time hoping for a fresh start. We will explore this pattern further in Chapter 6, incorporating participants' explanations of their return to alternative educational settings that worked for them and why.

Mini-Dropouts. We frequently encountered participants who, prior to officially dropping out, engaged in a pattern of multiple "mini-dropouts." These were students, like Jack, Trisha, and Yolanda, who stopped going to school for consecutive days, or sometimes weeks, then returned only to stop again. Although these periods of staying out of school may not have been long enough to be officially reported as a dropout event, the constant stopping and starting of school was so disruptive to their learning that it led to nearly the same academic results as officially and permanently dropping out, namely, course failure and insufficient credits accumulated toward graduation. When asked, "What were you thinking at this time?" a number replied to the effect, "I wasn't really thinking."

Interestingly, we did not see a consistent connection between when students started to skip school and how quickly they dropped out altogether. Some students experienced attendance problems in late elementary or early middle grades, yet persevered well into high school. Conversely, some high school students did not commence skipping classes until 10th or 11th grade, then dropped out within the year.

CONCLUSION

The patterns presented in this chapter, particularly the four phases of dropping out, provide a framework for exploring the dropping out process. Across the next several chapters we delve further into the multiple sources of disengagement from school—the initial phase in this often-lengthy process. We then examine how subsequent phases of the dropping out process unfold over time, culminating in what young people often perceive to be a tipping point—a decisive event or realization that ends their participation in school.

This framework underscores the importance of identifying and addressing disengagement factors while the student is still in an early phase of dropping out and has not yet started skipping lots of classes. Increased truancy associated with the third phase is of particular concern because, as a group, chronically truant students are less responsive to interventions than occasionally truant students (McKinney, 2013). In later chapters we examine more closely the causal antecedents to truancy and how truancy is deeply connected to dropping out.

While prevention and early intervention are key, schools should not give up on more chronically truant students. Even after routinely skipping and failing multiple courses, a surprising number of interviewees continued to attend high school (albeit sporadically) rather than dropping out altogether. These slow faders had something keeping them tenuously attached to their identities as students; this attachment provides ongoing opportunities for school intervention and support despite youths' seeming lack of interest in school, inability to succeed, or both.

In contrast, other participants left school precipitously. These accelerated leavers often faced significant personal challenges and departed within such a compressed time frame that schools had few opportunities to intervene. Stepping in to assist these students seems like a daunting, nearly impossible challenge for schools. In the final chapter we argue that through a range of student-centered policies and practices, educators can work to keep more of these young people, both slow faders and accelerated leavers, connected to school.

CHAPTER 2

Early School Years

Elementary? Yeah, I looked forward to school then. I liked seeing
friends. I was able to do all the work. —Xavier

In gathering oral histories from youths who had dropped out, we were
curious to learn when they had first started to lose interest in school
and why. In elementary grades, did these youths experience learning,
social, or behavioral issues that set the stage for later difficulties? Were
they unhappy with school from the start, or did a sense of disenchantment set in later? We were surprised to learn that almost all of the
young people we interviewed enjoyed elementary school, and that,
for most, factors creating an initial disengagement from school were
not yet salient. This chapter examines themes from early school years,
grades K–5, sharing the perspectives of the six young people we follow
throughout the book.

POSITIVE EARLY EXPERIENCES

In contrast to their later attitudes, almost all of the youths we interviewed held fond memories of elementary school. While they could not
always recall specific early learning tasks or instructional approaches,
they readily could describe their feelings about elementary school environments and learning contexts. These recollections were overwhelm-
ingly positive. When asked to rate school experiences on a five-point
scale, almost all participants (86%) assigned a favorable rating (a "4"
or a "5") to early elementary years (K–2nd grade); about 76% gave favorable ratings to late elementary years (3rd–5th grades). As Figure 2.1
shows, ratings for middle and high school were markedly less positive.
(The uptick in ratings for 11th and 12th grades is due largely to the
inclusion of young people who previously had dropped out but then
returned to a new educational setting they rated favorably.)

Figure 2.1. Percentage of Participants Rating School Favorably*

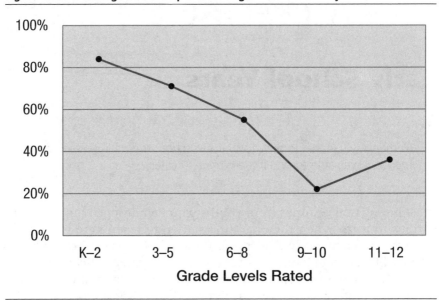

Grade Levels Rated

*Favorable ratings defined as a "4" or a "5" on a five-point scale. ($N = 39$–53); N of raters declines in high school due to some youths not attending at this point.

Early positive feelings toward school reflected three important themes: personal relationships with teachers, peer supports, and engaging learning activities.

Personal Relationships with Teachers

When encouraged to discuss classroom and learning experiences at the elementary level, youth interviewees frequently focused on their personal relationships with teachers, as opposed to lesson content or learning tasks. Positive feelings toward their elementary school teachers abounded, with many youths making comments such as the following:

> Mrs. Peterson was my favorite teacher. She was caring, you know, because at the time I was—I guess they diagnosed me with problems, issues. She treated everybody the same. . . . She was White, but she never treated us by race. She never gave one kid more favors than the rest of the class. . . . Sometimes I would come to school sad. I could talk to her. I felt like I could trust her. —Yolanda

Most who recalled early academic struggles felt supported by their teachers and other school staff. They especially noted the one-on-one attention they received from either teachers or tutors as being helpful when facing a learning challenge.

Often, the youths we interviewed remembered their favorite elementary teachers showing interest in them as individuals. These teachers not only supported students academically, but also made an effort to know their special interests and needs. For example, Yolanda was grateful that her favorite teacher understood her unstable family situation (she lived with an aunt who struggled to care for her) and the emotional fragility that came along with this, reaching out when Yolanda needed extra support. Others remembered their favorite elementary teacher as being particularly sensitive to their academic struggles, conveying emotional understanding and acceptance along with learning supports. Still others remembered just enjoying the general warmth, kindness, and interest that elementary teachers offered.

These kinds of personal interactions with teachers are significant because they can positively influence engagement in learning and commitment to school (Farrington et al., 2012). However, the reverse is also true: When young people lack positive personal connections to their teachers, their motivation, engagement, and school performance suffer. We will consider negative aspects of teacher–student relationships in later chapters when we examine participants' middle and high school years.

Peer Supports

The youths we interviewed expressed their enjoyment of elementary school in terms of social connections—making friends, playing at recess, and interacting throughout the day. Classroom tasks and activities were exciting, in part because students engaged in them collaboratively with peers as well as with the teacher:

> When I was in 1st grade probably up until 5th grade I'd say I really looked forward to going to school. Because, to me, it was just a time to hang out with my friends. . . . Fifth grade was before, you know, being too nerdy made you unpopular. And it was also before everybody was worried about, you know, what everybody looked like or how you dressed—because we were kids enjoying having time with our friends. And to me that was a treasurable time in my life. —Jack

For most, peer connections seemed less predicated on social status or academic ability in elementary school than in later grades. In particular, students who faced learning or other personal challenges still felt very much a part of their class in elementary school.

Engaging Learning Activities

In addition to positive associations with elementary school teachers and peers, youth participants recalled enjoying learning activities when they were younger. "Learning was fun back then" and "I looked forward to learning something new every day" were widely shared sentiments. When asked to recall a favorite classroom experience, they often referred to hands-on activities such as conducting science experiments, exploring subjects on a computer, or taking field trips. Positive classroom experiences frequently were also connected to opportunities for personal expression through art, music, drama, or writing:

> My favorite classroom activity, besides reading, was writing. We'd start off every day in 3rd grade with writing. We'd just write about how our day is going or do a free write on something. And just to be able to sit there and write everything out and not feel like I was gonna get in trouble for something I wrote about—that's what I liked. —Jack

In line with research on student engagement, these kinds of active learning opportunities appeared to nurture engagement in learning and strengthen participants' confidence in themselves as competent learners (Pianta, Hamre, & Allen, 2012).

Early Positive Mindsets

Academic mindset refers to attitudes toward learning and school, educational goals, and beliefs about one's own academic abilities. Research suggests academic mindsets can have a profound effect on motivation to learn, intellectual effort, and learning outcomes (Farrington et al., 2012). Dweck (2006) points to two contrasting views of intelligence: *fixed*, where ability is seen as innate and unchanging; and *dynamic*, where ability is viewed as a quality that can change and grow with effort. She argues that students who attribute school success to innate intelligence (fixed mindset) instead of effort (dynamic, or growth, mindset) are more likely to shrink away from new learning challenges. When prompted to think about themselves as learners during elementary school years, many youth interviewees depicted growth mindsets at this stage, describing positive scenarios of learning to read and write, conquering arithmetic, and immersing themselves in creative activities. Some, like Callie, vividly recalled a strong sense of engagement and accomplishment they felt at this early stage of their education:

> Later in elementary school I was learning more and faster, and I was getting more excited about middle school and high school and what I could do in the future. I started learning better math and better writing and better reading and started learning about science, and I was just so excited to learn in elementary school! —Callie

As we explore in the next chapter, interviewees' mindsets dramatically shifted in a negative direction during middle school.

EMERGING SCHOOL CHALLENGES

Although youths portrayed their early school years as mostly positive and engaging, this time period also marked the emergence of academic and behavioral challenges for some. Occasionally these challenges were prominent, but more often they constituted a small strand of the overall school experience that later would grow to dominate and undermine life at school.

Learning Difficulties

By the time they finished middle school, almost all the youths we interviewed faced significant academic difficulties. For some, these difficulties seemed to originate in elementary school and then magnify over time. A few faced early learning challenges that were serious in nature, requiring them to receive special education services. Both Derrick and Trisha were representative of this subpopulation of young people who struggled academically at an early age. Derrick's early difficulties with reading were particularly pronounced and consequential:

> I don't think I, like, wanted to read in elementary school. . . . I wasn't a very good reader. That's probably why I wasn't interested. Like, in elementary school they made all the kids go into a reading class at the start of the day, and there's different levels of reading and all that. And I was always in the low levels, like, not a very good reader. —Derrick

Trisha was one of the few youths who remembered actively disliking early elementary school. Judging from her narrative, she was significantly disengaged from elementary school due, at least in part, to her diagnosed learning issues and to being retained:

> I always hated school. Well, preschool wasn't so bad because we got to play most of the time. It was more once I got into elementary school—1st grade and on. . . . School was never really for me. I got held back in 1st grade. I had a hard time learning to read, and they—they said that they wanted to make sure that I got down all of the basic skills that every other 1st-grader had . . . so that's why they held me back. —Trisha

Other students recalled having difficulties conquering basic math operations related to multiplication, fractions, or decimals. These early difficulties grasping numeric concepts may have contributed to a later increase in anxiety about math and subsequent learning and performance challenges (Ramirez, Gunderson, Levine, & Beilock, 2013). Xavier exemplifies the connection between early math learning challenges and math anxiety:

> I always knew I was a strong, good reader, but when it came to math, I wasn't as good. It wasn't that I thought I wasn't smart enough. It's just that I couldn't remember how to do a problem. When I got called on in class, I don't know, it just became a fog as I tried to remember the numbers. I knew the answer. . . . But when I was under pressure, I couldn't do it. —Xavier

In the same breath as they discussed general learning problems, a number of youths we interviewed also recollected their elementary school teachers or tutors providing one-on-one help in both math and reading. They almost always remembered this extra instructional support in a positive light: Students who received individual attention believed it bolstered their confidence, improved their skills, and increased their learning. Ultimately, early literacy and numeracy challenges did not appear to impact most youths' overall enjoyment of and engagement in elementary school. However, for some, these seemingly small challenges set the stage for more serious academic problems to come in middle and high school.

In contrast, the majority who struggled in middle school did not recall having substantial learning difficulties or receiving any special education support in elementary school. Often their reported learning challenges revolved around a particular skills deficit, one that did not seem to seriously impact them at an early stage. For example, some remembered struggling with understanding more complex texts (chapter books or nonfiction texts) or with writing and spelling assignments.

Behavior Issues

For a few participants, mostly boys, early behavior problems played a role in shaping negative attitudes toward school. They perceived school as a conflict-filled environment where they might not be able to control themselves and where punishment was a certainty. For this small subset of young people, even elementary school was not quite so fondly remembered. Xavier, struggling from an early age with anger issues, recollected his elementary school behavior challenges in this way:

> I was always talking when I wasn't supposed to, and I had an anger management problem. The first time I got suspended was 3rd grade. I was getting bullied, and I was tired of being bullied, so I kinda hit a kid hard with a book. We both got suspended for about the same amount of time. . . . I didn't really think it was fair. . . . I missed a lot of recess because I was always in trouble, I guess. —Xavier

Attendance Issues

A small number of youths also admitted to having attendance problems in elementary grades: About 8% of young people we interviewed had experimented with skipping school by the time they were 11 years old, and 16% by the time they were 12 years old (it is important to note that most of the 12-year-olds attended 6th grade in a middle school, a context where they might readily observe older students who skipped classes). This small subset of youths essentially had moved from initial disengagement to the second phase of the dropping out process, early skipping.

These young school avoiders were a distinct group whose lives and school experiences often were disrupted by family circumstances or individual mental health problems, such as anxiety and depression. During their elementary years, some already had experienced serious family dysfunction or had spent time in foster care. These participants also were more likely to have manifested serious behavioral or learning problems at an early age. We should emphasize that this very early skipping behavior was relatively rare; our six profiled youths represented the much more common pattern of commencing to skip classes after 6th grade.

Academic Behaviors

Academic behaviors are highly visible student traits that support school success: showing up on time, paying attention, participating in class, completing assignments, and persisting in the face of difficult learning tasks (Duckworth, 2016; Farrington et al., 2012).[1] We often think of these traits in conjunction with the demands of secondary school, but clearly the foundation for successful academic behaviors is developed earlier. A number of youths reflected that they had failed to develop this important foundation, engaging in counterproductive academic behaviors while still in elementary grades. Some portrayed themselves as not really trying, coasting through elementary school because it was "easy." By their own accounts, they successfully avoided new challenges and instead developed negative academic behaviors like being tardy, not doing homework, or not completing in-class assignments. Interviews revealed that the majority of interviewees had lived either with a single working parent, with non-English-speaking parents, or in unstable households; in many cases, therefore, the family's ability to support positive academic behaviors, like completing homework, may have been limited.

Interviewees remember suffering few consequences for poor academic habits in their elementary years. However, as we will discuss further in the next chapter, when these youths carried the same counterproductive behaviors into middle school, they (from their perspective) suddenly were confronted with negative outcomes they could not so easily ignore—test and course failure, parental and teacher disapproval, and self- and peer judgments about their abilities. These outcomes, in turn, would further influence their academic mindsets in a negative direction.

Negative Mindsets

By late elementary school, students are developmentally primed to make ability comparisons as a way to understand their own capacities (Dijkstra, Kuyper, van der Werf, Buunk, & van der Zee, 2008). For struggling students especially, this is a critical time period: Without proactive interventions and appropriate supports, they are likely to view their academic struggles as evidence of inherent limitations. Over time, this negative mindset can feed anxiety, damage motivation to learn, create anger and frustration, and lead to behavioral issues. To explore youth participants' perspectives on academic mindsets and beliefs about intelligence, we asked them to share with us any early learning challenges they remembered, how they dealt with these challenges, and how they felt about their math and reading abilities at different stages of their schooling. A complex and somewhat contradictory picture emerged of their early mindsets.

Most youths we interviewed professed to embrace, even when they were young, a growth mindset, believing that application of effort was the key to "growing your brain" (Dweck, 2006) and to doing well in school. A number believed, in retrospect, that lack of effort, rather than lack of intelligence, explained their learning difficulties; they simply hadn't applied themselves enough. Yet some of these same young people were also quick to equate their math difficulties with a fixed ability that did *not* grow with effort. Like Trisha, they expressed the sentiment that they had "never been good in math," implying that as far back as they could remember, their abilities were subpar and there was not much they could do to change their circumstances:

> I remember when I was younger I just didn't think I was good in math. I just didn't think I could do it, you know? —Trisha

Interestingly, however, the majority of interviewees could not recall specific early math challenges that led them to see themselves as "no good in math." In response to the questions, *"Do you remember how you felt about your abilities to do reading, math, and other assignments?"* and *"How were you doing academically at this time?"* most youths characterized their math capabilities as acceptable during elementary school. However, because so many then floundered in middle school math, we suspect that even those who did not acknowledge early difficulties actually faced math learning challenges that had not been fully addressed.

As a group, youths were more likely to recall specific problems with reading or writing rather than with math in elementary grades. However, unlike with math, very few cast their early literacy struggles as arising from fixed abilities. This difference may have to do partially with the process of learning to read: Phonics and decoding represent an initial challenge, but once these skills develop, students tend to see themselves as good readers, even if they subsequently do not strengthen comprehension skills (McKenna, Kear, & Ellsworth, 1995). We examine changes over time in youths' attitudes toward reading and mathematics in Chapters 3 and 4.

About one fourth of the young people we interviewed remembered specific math-related experiences in elementary school that shaped their perspectives, both positive and negative, on their learning abilities. Ability comparisons with peers played a central role in this process, particularly regarding the rapidity with which they mastered math facts and operations. Those with a retrospectively *negative view* of their early math abilities recalled being "slow" to master these skills, compared with their classmates:

> We used to have these time sheets. One times five, two times five, you know, and they used to have this little competition where everybody was on a different times table. . . . I was stuck on that a good 6, 7 months. Everybody went past me, so I knew then that math wasn't a good fit. —Xavier

Timed multiplication tests, in particular, seemed to invite young people we interviewed to make unwelcome comparisons. As the excerpt above illustrates, those who struggled to develop this particular skill interpreted the tests as clear evidence that they were not as smart or capable as their peers—that they were simply "no good in math."

We suspect that literacy challenges also had a negative impact on mindset, leading to a more static view of intelligence. While they might not couch their problems so openly in terms of their innate abilities, students like Derrick and Trisha, who faced early reading difficulties, clearly perceived that they weren't progressing as fast as others. As their earlier quotes illustrate, they became discouraged at a young age about their abilities, withdrew their effort, or settled for just getting by with minimal effort.

CONCLUSION

One of the most surprising findings from our investigation of pathways to dropping out is that most of the young people we interviewed began their school careers on a promising note. By and large, these youths recalled enjoying elementary school, especially the primary grades. Some remembered struggling with early learning challenges, but at this stage they also, for the most part, felt supported by their teachers and other school personnel. Their stories reveal how important positive personal relationships with teachers, positive peer interaction, and engaging learning activities were to their enjoyment of school. We will argue in subsequent chapters that these features of the learning environment remain critical to student engagement in secondary school as well.

Against this positive backdrop, interviewees also revealed ominous signs of potential problems to come. Some students, like Yolanda, faced family conflict and instability that affected their ability to fully participate in and enjoy school, even at this early stage. Others, like Xavier, had behavioral issues that constantly got them into trouble. Still others experienced academic difficulties that may not have been adequately addressed at the time. Finally, by late elementary school, we saw the emergence of counterproductive mindsets, especially regarding math. In the next chapter we will explore how emerging negative mindsets become solidified in the middle school years, encouraging problem behaviors that carry youths further along pathways to dropping out.

CHAPTER 3

Middle School Challenges

My problems with school really started in 7th and 8th grades.
Middle school kinda just got dull, you know? —Xavier

One might expect a bumpy transition as students move from the familiar, comfortable confines of elementary school to the larger, unfamiliar, and more complex institutional settings that typically characterize secondary education. Researchers have long recognized that this transition is associated with a slump in academic engagement and performance (Eccles, Lord, & Midgley, 1991; Pianta et al., 2012). Yet while their interest in school wanes, most students still manage to pass their required courses and to graduate.

For many youths in our study, middle school marked the beginning of an academic decline that did not subside. It is as if these young people stumble and lose their academic footing in middle school, are unable to regain their balance, and continue to lose academic ground year after year. Unlike their peers who continue to make progress toward graduation, these students appear to lack the skills, supports, or confidence needed to negotiate these setbacks, never quite figuring out how to clamber back. Instead, they continue a downward slide, so that by the time they reach high school (if they reach high school), they are well down the pathway to dropping out.

What happens in the middle grades to cause these youths to stumble and pull away from school? As others have noted, multiple factors, both internal and external to school, influence how the dropping out process unfolds (National Research Council, 2004; Rumberger, 2011). A subset of young people brings personal challenges to school, such as homelife difficulties or mental health problems. These factors negatively affect their ability to study and make progress, thus interfering with their long-term educational trajectories (Freudenberg & Ruglis, 2007). We recognize the important role such nonschool factors play in the dropping out process, and discuss this topic separately in Chapter 5. In this chapter we continue to focus on school-related factors, examining the major themes and issues associated with early phases of the dropping out process. These overarching themes include the following:

- New academic challenges and expectations
- Negative mindsets
- Unsupportive learning environments
- Early and unchecked skipping

NEW ACADEMIC CHALLENGES AND EXPECTATIONS

Middle school academic expectations came as a shock to most of the youths we interviewed: "It got hard" was a common refrain. As described below, they perceived middle school as "too hard" for three distinct reasons: (1) they lacked the literacy and math skills required in order to be successful; (2) they displayed the emergence of decidedly fixed mindsets regarding their intellectual capabilities, especially in math; and (3) they had not adequately understood or developed the academic behaviors needed for school success at the secondary level.

Lack of Literacy and Math Skills

As we learned in Chapter 2, a number of youth participants experienced early struggles in math, reading, or both, and likely entered middle school with unaddressed learning challenges. Placed in mainstream classes, they complained that the pace of instruction was "too fast" and that they were unable to keep up. This fundamental mismatch between youths' skill levels and middle school coursework expectations contributed to poor academic outcomes, which in turn created unresolved student frustration and even anger. Struggling students like Derrick sought ways to avoid these aversive circumstances by tuning out or acting up:

> I liked coming to middle school at the start . . . and then some of the teachers and me just didn't get along good. I didn't understand the work, and I couldn't get all the help that I needed, and that's when I started not liking school. —Derrick

As discussed in the previous chapter, students' relatively high engagement during their early school years may have helped mediate their learning issues. Lagging behind in basic skills may have been uncomfortable at times during elementary school, but there were many other aspects of school that struggling students could latch onto and enjoy during this period—caring teachers, creative activities, hands-on projects, and recess with peers. In middle school, with the increased emphasis on grades and tests, their lower proficiency in core academic skills became more visible and consequential. At the same time, the level of individual support available to these academically vulnerable students declined. Additionally, as we will explore later in the chapter, there were few things in middle school to engage or motivate struggling students to learn.

The Math Tripwire

Of all the subjects youth interviewees discussed, mathematics stood out as the one most likely to have tripped them up in the middle grades. Nearly 70% mentioned math as a problematic class for them by middle or early high school. Many connected their disenchantment with school to struggles with math, especially in pre-algebra and algebra classes. Even students like Callie, who had done well academically up to this point, felt upended by algebra assignments:

> I had to do a study group. I had to get all this extra help from my mom and from my sister, and I was still not getting it. . . . I was getting really upset because I couldn't try any harder. If the class had gone a little bit slower, I probably would have done a lot better. —Callie

The traditional sequenced approach to math instruction left some youths floundering; those who failed to grasp math concepts in a timely way found their class advancing while they fell further behind. In addition, math difficulties seemed to reinforce a fixed view of math abilities (Boaler, 2015), with students believing that if they did not "get it" now, then they never would.

Academic Behaviors Needed for Success

Certain *academic behaviors*—getting to class on time, paying attention, participating in class, completing assignments, and studying for tests—are central to school success (Farrington et al., 2012). By their own accounts, many youths we interviewed did not develop these key academic behaviors in elementary school and, as a result, were unprepared for middle school. They portrayed themselves as either unaware of the connection between good academic habits, learning outcomes, and grades, or simply unconcerned at that time with doing well academically.

Homework Issues. Middle school independent work requirements presented significant stumbling blocks for youth participants for a variety of reasons. As described in the previous chapter, some confessed that they had avoided doing homework while in elementary school but had suffered no serious consequences as a result. In middle school, the consequences were immediate and sometimes severe—a failing grade. There also may have been an element of learned helplessness, promoting the development of counterproductive behaviors: Some interviewees admitted that if something seemed hard or unfamiliar and an adult was not nearby to help, they simply quit without really trying. Trisha noted:

> Yeah—I never turned in my work when I was in elementary school. No one was home to help me, so when I didn't understand something or didn't have supplies around to do a project, I just didn't do the assignments. I just followed the same pattern in middle and high school, but then I failed because of it. —Trisha

New Demands, Waning Effort. Many youth participants seemed caught off guard by the increased level of academic effort and independent work required of them in middle school. Rather than attempting to meet the new expectations, students like Derrick, Yolanda, Trisha, and Xavier retreated. Here is Trisha remembering homework issues:

> I failed classes in math. In 8th grade it was pre-algebra, but it was just because I wasn't doing my homework and turning it in because I didn't want to. I don't know why. I just didn't. I didn't really like homework in general. It wasn't like I was a rebellious kid or anything. —Trisha

Why did these struggling students avoid asking for help with homework or other assignments? As we explore later in this chapter, their perceptions of teachers as unsupportive and fears of being judged or humiliated in front of peers militated against taking this seemingly obvious step on their own behalf. In addition, as described below, *negative mindsets* also figured in their passive responses to learning challenges.

NEGATIVE MINDSETS

The young people we interviewed often reported that their views of intelligence evolved over time. Most currently subscribed to a dynamic mindset in which they saw effort (as opposed to native intelligence) as a crucial component of school success. However, when recollecting what they believed as young adolescents, most admitted they thought their abilities were fixed, especially in regard to math. As we saw in the previous chapter, this view of math ability as fixed had emerged among a few participants in elementary school; by the end of middle school this mindset was practically normative in the study group. It is important to note that the degree to which participants truly shifted from a fixed to a growth mindset over time remains unclear. Few were able to describe how, as more mature students returning to school, they had applied effort to achieve progress in math; most were silent on this topic, made vague references to "doing better," or directly contradicted themselves by admitting that they still felt "no good in math." These findings speak to the deep-seated nature of their negative mindsets.

In line with Dweck's (2006) research, young people holding a fixed view of their abilities withdrew effort in the face of middle school academic challenges, which, in turn, appeared to contribute to their disengagement from school. When these youths encountered difficulties in middle school, they often did not reach out to teachers for help, fearing that such exposure might further confirm for both student and teacher that the student was not "smart" enough to do the work. Inevitably, this avoidance strategy only worsened the situation. In line with the "frustration–self-esteem" model of truancy proposed by J. D. Finn (1989), many interviewees connected their negative learning experiences in middle school and resulting negative mindsets to their subsequent early truancy. Figure 3.1 depicts the sequence that moved them into Phase 2 of the dropping out process.

Figure 3.1. Steps to Skipping

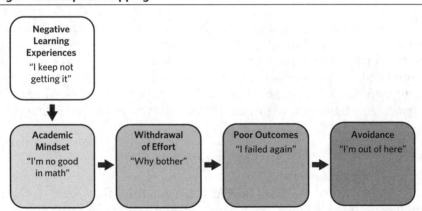

According to youth participants, some teachers tried to encourage and motivate them by saying, "You are smart—you can do this work." However, Dweck (2006) argues that praising or rewarding *innate ability*, as opposed to *effort*, can be counterproductive and actually lead to a reduction in student effort and learning. Similarly, simply being told they were bright did not help these youths overcome their negative view of their abilities, motivate them to work harder, or give them needed strategies to succeed.

Intertwining Factors

Course failure in middle school consistently has been found to be predictive of dropping out (Balfanz, Herzog, & Mac Iver, 2007), so it is not surprising that most youth participants reported failing one or more classes by 9th grade. Were inadequate academic skills and behaviors the main factor of their early disengagement from school? Or did other behaviors, such as intentional skipping of classes, precipitate poor academic behaviors, which in turn led to course failure?

In certain cases, truancy behavior seemed to come first: Some interviewees reported that they started skipping school primarily for social reasons, then felt there was no point in putting effort into classes they had missed. But in more instances the reverse appeared to occur: *Students' well-established academic problems both preceded and encouraged truancy.* Moreover, negative academic behaviors, including skipping classes, tended to arise in tandem with unresolved learning issues. Therefore, when young people we interviewed reported struggling in a subject, they did not necessarily distinguish between problems due to academic challenges and those due to their limited efforts and intentional absences. In determining primary causes for school disengagement, youths themselves had trouble disentangling these factors. Moreover, in many cases, certain aspects of the middle school learning environment appeared to encourage self-defeating academic behaviors, as described below.

UNSUPPORTIVE LEARNING ENVIRONMENTS

Research has linked various school environmental factors to student outcomes, including coursework completion and graduation. School climate, class size, classroom interactions, and teacher instructional choices all influence a student's engagement and academic behavior

(National Research Council, 2004; Neild, 2009). This section explores the connections between several key school environmental factors and middle school disengagement among youth participants.

Impersonal School Environment

Most youth participants perceived elementary school as a positive community in which teacher assistance was readily available. By contrast, they often perceived middle school as an uncaring, impersonal, and sometimes even explicitly unwelcoming environment in which students felt unwanted or lost. Common themes that emerged from their depictions of their middle school environments include:

- The challenge of adjusting to multiple classes and teachers made the school day difficult.
- The absence of friends and familiar faces made classes less fun.
- The sense that teachers did not know or care about students made students feel isolated.

Large class sizes and short time frames—typically less than an hour per class—hampered opportunities for students to get to know peers or teachers. For many, the sense of belonging to a classroom-based community vanished, leaving students feeling anonymous and alone in these large and ever-changing class settings:

> I thought I was prepared. . . . And I was like, "Yeah, this is gonna be easy!" But then, in 7th grade, instead of having only one teacher give you all the homework, it was each teacher giving you a little bit of homework. And then, you had to deal with all these different classes with all these different teachers . . . it was just . . . overwhelming. —Callie

Youths also reflected that the larger middle school classes tended to feel noisy and distracting, making it difficult to focus and learn. Others connected class sizes to an inability to get help when they needed it:

> At the time all the classes in middle school were overfull. So in my science class there were 34 students for one teacher. And that situation was just out of hand. You could never get one-on-one time with the teacher. Because when you go to raise your hand and ask a question, you're followed by 11 other people. —Jack

For some, the sense of anonymity and disconnection they experienced in middle school made it easier to slack off doing assignments and to start skipping classes that were not going well. A widely shared perception was that school personnel did not always notice or care whether students were absent or present.

Weak Personal Connection to Teachers

Researchers have linked students' social interactions with teachers to their level of engagement in learning and commitment to school (Croninger & Lee, 2001; Farrington et al., 2012). Similarly, the importance of having a connection to teachers surfaced in participant interviews as a central theme. When contrasting their elementary and secondary learning environments, interviewees focused on their relationships with teachers, mourning the loss of the kinds of positive personal connections they had experienced in elementary grades. Middle school teachers often were seen as distant, uninterested in knowing or helping students, or simply too busy to make themselves available:

> The teachers were not really enthused about their job . . . and when you go into a classroom, you're coming from being a kid and in a happy environment, going in middle school into a dull environment, and you can just feel the vibes the teacher gives off in the room. Most teachers I had were kinda mean in middle school. —Xavier

Some struggling students also had the sense that teachers preferred to help the more capable students—those who were, in Trisha's words, "more special":

> Honestly, I don't think the teachers really had expectations for anybody other than students that were special to them because there were so many of us that I don't think that they put expectations on each and every one of us. I just felt like they wouldn't have enough time to get to me, let alone everybody else, or even know who we were. —Trisha

When students encountered academic difficulties, weak connections to teachers seemed to prevent many from asking for help. What did they think would happen if they asked the teacher for help? Commonly, they believed the teacher would:

- Chastise them for not paying enough attention
- Become impatient or sarcastic
- Repeat the same explanation or instructions that students did not understand the first time
- Discover students' limitations and judge them negatively

Lack of Individualized Support

Youth participants with learning challenges lamented the lack of individual supports available to them in middle school. They most frequently described their unaddressed learning difficulties and subsequent disengagement in conjunction with math, but similar problems surfaced in other classes as well. Sometimes participants directly connected the size of the class to a lack of individual attention, but many also portrayed teachers as unable or unwilling to differentiate approaches and explanations to meet individual needs. In response to students' questions, a teacher might repeat the explanation, direct them to reading material, or ask them to ask another student. The latter was often not an effective approach because a fellow student might not be willing or able to help:

> The teacher just didn't understand how everybody's not on the same level. I was listening and everything, but I just wanted her to say the explanation again or something, but the teacher just wouldn't. She's telling me instead to ask somebody next to me. That person is not telling me. —Callie

When struggling students received individualized attention, it sometimes made a huge difference in their mindset, motivation, and effort. Here is Yolanda's recollection of a favorite middle school teacher, in whose class she did well, in contrast to her other classes:

> She actually, like, took her time. You know, she wasn't one of the teachers that got irritated by your hand being raised or by questions and stuff. Like, she didn't mind repeating herself. —Yolanda

Disengaging Instruction

Students who drop out often claim they were "bored" and "turned off" by their classroom experience (America's Promise Alliance, 2014; Bridgeland et al., 2006). Many of our youth participants said the same, but what exactly did they mean by "bored"? We explored this question by asking them to describe specific instructional practices or contexts associated with classes they disliked or found boring, versus those they enjoyed or found interesting. What follows are discussions of some aspects of classroom instruction that students commonly perceived as detrimental to their engagement and learning.

Reliance on Lecturing. Interviewees typically disliked classes that were lecture-based, and recalled having a difficult time following this instructional style. They found this kind of passive learning boring and wanted to be more actively engaged in class. When teachers lectured, students often tuned out:

> I was also bored because the teachers make you sit there and listen while they read. And they have a monotone voice, and it's just, like, putting me to sleep. —Callie

Course Content Disconnected from Students' Lives. Interviewees routinely complained that they felt no connection between what they were being asked to learn and why it was relevant or important to their lives. When they labeled a task "boring" or too challenging, this often meant they could not see a larger purpose for understanding new concepts or abstract ideas:

> I wouldn't be using anything I learned in school out in everyday life. Like advanced math and geometry and all that. It's not like I'm going to be a rocket scientist. —Derrick

Worksheets and Independent Work. Students lamented that they did not understand material sufficiently to complete independent work, whether worksheets in class or homework:

> We got this new math teacher, and I didn't like her at all. Like, she didn't even teach us. She'd give us a worksheet, and she'd tell us about the worksheet, and we'd sit there the whole class, and she would maybe help us a little bit. —Derrick

They fell into a pattern of not completing independent work, and their grades suffered.

One-Size-Fits-All Instruction. Generic content and pacing of lessons created conditions conducive to disengagement. Students who lacked necessary background knowledge, missed part of an instructional sequence, or needed more time to process new learning seemed to fall off a moving instructional train that did not stop for them. These students might continue to attend class for a while but not understand the material, resulting in feelings of boredom, frustration, and even anger. Earlier we alluded to problems with generic instruction in math, but learning and disengagement issues connected to undifferentiated instruction occurred in other subjects as well. For example, Derrick participated in special reading classes through most of middle school:

> Finally they graduated me out of the reading class and said I was a good reader. I thought that reading class was really boring. . . . I just don't understand why I needed it. —Derrick

In practically the same breath, Derrick admitted that throughout middle and high school he "didn't really read any books or even remember nothing." His reading classes may have focused on developing certain skills, but apparently did not address Derrick's individual underlying issues—his negative mindset regarding his abilities and his well-developed aversion to reading for pleasure or for depth of understanding.

Engaging Instruction

Participants most frequently associated positive classroom experiences with opportunities for personal expression through art, music, drama, or writing. When asked to recall a favorite classroom experience, they also referred often to "hands-on" activities that allowed them to learn through doing rather than sitting and listening. Even a student as turned off by middle school as Derrick found a positive connection to learning through hands-on science:

> I always liked 7th-grade science because we did hands-on activities. I remember one time in science we got to dissect a frog to learn about organs. And then we put some tissue under the microscope, and I thought that was pretty cool. —Derrick

In addition, a number of interviewees mentioned being engaged in projects or activities that they had a choice in selecting. However, these opportunities for choice, self-expression, and active learning occurred largely at the elementary level (described in Chapter 2) and seemed, from participants' perspectives, to virtually disappear during middle school. *Strikingly, most young people we interviewed could not recall a single engaging learning activity during all of middle school.*

These themes of engaging versus disengaging learning experiences align with research indicating a fundamental mismatch between middle school instructional approaches and the developmental needs of adolescents (Eccles et al., 1991; National Research Council, 2004). For example, Pianta and Allen (2008) argue that developmentally appropriate instruction at the secondary level should provide ample opportunities for peer interaction, autonomous decisionmaking, and skills development. Participants' stories suggest that such opportunities shrink over time, with middle school instructional approaches emphasizing mandated assignments for all, decreased student choice, competitive grading, and limited interaction with peers. This mismatch between adolescent developmental needs and middle school curriculum and instruction appears to depress student engagement and learning (Eccles & Roeser, 2009), which, in turn, acts as a further catalyst toward truancy.

Previously in this chapter we explored connections between negative learning experiences, negative mindsets, withdrawal of effort, and early skipping behaviors. Because experimental skipping of classes is such a critical precursor to more serious truancy, we now take a closer look at the origins of and common school responses to this behavior.

EARLY AND UNCHECKED SKIPPING BEHAVIOR

Thus far we have explored how middle school frequently marked initial disengagement from school, the first phase of the dropping out process. During this time period, many study participants also entered the next phase of the process: early skipping. Based on interview information, we estimated that almost half started skipping school at or before the age of 14.

A pattern of skipping classes over time is the hallmark of a student heading toward dropping out; almost all students who leave school without graduating have had prior attendance problems over a period of time (McKinney, 2013, Rumberger, 2011). Interviewees said they often started skipping one or two classes and did so only sporadically at first, increasing the frequency of their absences over time. Both Derrick and Xavier entered this early skipping phase in middle school. Callie, Yolanda, and Trisha followed suit in 9th grade.

Spontaneous vs. Targeted Skipping

Sometimes early skipping behavior was not associated with any particular class, appearing to be less preplanned and more spontaneous in nature. On the spur of the moment and in response to social enticements from peers, a student might decide to take an extra hour for lunch. Frequently, however, skipping was intentional and targeted: A student decided ahead of time not to attend a particular class for a specific reason. Typically, the youths failed to see the relevance of course content and embraced the idea that it "didn't matter" if they flunked a class in middle school because grades "didn't count." In addition, intentional early skipping of certain classes appeared connected to learning and academic performance issues: Students chose to skip the class in which they had trouble mastering the material (most often math or science). When the learning context became aversive enough, avoidance of the class, even though it might carry negative consequences in the long term, seemed a preferable choice in the moment:

> The work just started getting hard and I just didn't understand and all that. So I was just like, "I can't do this, so I'm not going to waste my time coming in and sitting here and feeling dumb the whole time." I never did homework or anything. Probably I started skipping to not get called on. —Derrick

Regardless of whether skipping class was planned or spontaneous, it was almost always a social rather than a solitary experience. Hanging out with friends who also were also skipping (or out of school altogether) presented an enticing alternative to being in a class.

School Responses to Skipping

Most participants initially were afraid of the consequences they might receive from parents or school for skipping class, and their apprehensions acted to curb skipping behavior. However, once skipping behaviors commenced, consequences were not always immediately forthcoming, especially if students confined skipping to a single class. They worked diligently to conceal absences by intercepting school notifications and thus were often (according to interviewees) successful in delaying parental knowledge of their absences. Moreover, numerous participants reported that their school did not consistently inform parents of unexcused absences as they occurred. Later in the term, of course, students usually experienced unpleasant academic consequences, such as a poor progress report or, ultimately, a failing grade. However, these delayed consequences did little to discourage skipping.

Even when consequences such as detention occurred more immediately, students often perceived them as meaningless and therefore did not respond with a change in behavior. Derrick's characterization of the school response to his early skipping was not atypical:

> I'd have to stay in a little room at lunch, you know, so I wouldn't be able to skip during lunch. And I was happy to be with my friend, so I don't know why the school would do that. Like, it was kinda dumb because my friend was there, so I wouldn't care if I was there. —Derrick

The unintended consequences of sanctions were most evident in cases in which schools (reportedly) responded to unexcused absences by suspending the student for a few days. As several youths explained, such suspensions gave them an extended "vacation" from school— exactly what they were aiming for.

CONCLUSION

Middle school marked an educational turning point for most participants: By the end of this time period most had ceased to enjoy school, and many had started to lose confidence in themselves as learners. In this chapter we covered a multiplicity of factors that started them on their pathways to dropping out. Some of these factors were individual: Participants exhibited unresolved learning challenges, inadequate study skills, or both. Additional factors, however, were school-based: large classes, one-size-fits-all instruction, lack of individual and targeted support, multiple teachers, and few opportunities to develop trust and a personal connection with those teachers.

Traditionally, researchers and educators have focused on the transition into high school as a critical juncture for supporting successful student outcomes (Neild, 2009). However, youths' stories affirm that for many vulnerable students, middle school is a critical transition that can launch them onto a pathway to dropping out. Participants painted a complex picture of how middle school disengagement was set in motion and then reinforced through a confluence of factors. Typically, academic behavior, mindset, and school performance issues became deeply intertwined over time, leading many to commence skipping classes. Nowhere was this dynamic more evident than in math.

Because missing class inevitably worsens this dynamic, early middle school appears to be a critical time for intense, comprehensive intervention. Youths' narratives make abundantly clear the need for educators and counselors to look beyond the outward manifestations of disengagement (not turning in work, missing classes) to understand

and disrupt the dynamic generating counterproductive behavior. An effective intervention will explore and address an *individual student's particular needs* with regard to mindsets, skills gaps, learning issues, and academic behaviors. Moreover, stories from struggling students point to the need to examine *traditional pedagogical approaches* that may promote disengagement. In the final chapter, we describe schoolwide *prevention policies and practices* that proactively encourage a student's sense of connection to school and engagement in learning.

Yolanda's Story

Yolanda is an African American young woman with a commanding, cheerful presence who is remarkably open about her painful childhood. Having lost her mother at a young age to drug addiction, Yolanda lived with her aunt through most of elementary school, but in middle school was placed in a group foster home. She experienced difficulties with her peers in this setting and felt that students at the large urban schools she attended picked on her for being a skilled reader. Although she did fairly well academically in the middle grades, she admitted getting involved with the "wrong crowd" in early high school. She eventually took up a life on the streets as a teen prostitute.

Early School Years

We were raising chicks in our kindergarten class. And there was a big glass. It was a hot glass I guess 'cause to keep it hot for the baby chicks and stuff in there. That was, like, the best year of school for me. I wish I could go back to just return, rewind the hands of time and go back there. I think those were the best years because you're just small and little and you just play around all the time. And you're just so happy.

I've always liked reading. That was my thing. Reading was easy for me. Man, it was really easy. I guess when I was young I really was always reading. Like, my aunt said that her and my uncle had caught me with a picture book, and they thought that I was really young though, and they thought that I was reading the pictures, but come to find out they was looking over me, and I guess I was reading the words, like, sounding them out and stuff on my own. So I've always been good at reading; like, that's been my good thing to do. Kids used to tease me because they said I used to show off, I guess. And I wasn't. I was just really good at reading, you know? I just always wanted to read out loud. Every time we—something like a subject or something, then the teacher would be like, "Who wants to read out loud?" I'll have my hand up like, "Oh, I wanna read. I wanna read." And I would always read every day. Kids are really mean. I honestly feel that kids in elementary school are a lot meaner than your middle school kids and high school kids. They tease you, they make song rhymes about you, yeah.

Mrs. Peterson was my favorite teacher. She was caring, you know, because at the time I was—I guess they diagnosed me with problems, issues, you know how that goes. She treated everybody the same. She never treated us by color, you know, because she was White, but she never treated us by race. She never gave one kid more favors than the rest of the class. We all had a share opportunity. Sometimes I would come to school sad. I could talk to her. I felt like I could trust her. She was really cool. Actually she—sometimes I would forget she was just our 2nd-grade teacher. That's how cool she was.

I switched schools in 3rd grade. My aunt switched my schools I guess because I was having too many conflicts at that school. Kids picking on me and stuff. My aunt, she believed in education. She believed that as long as I had this, I could make it in life, you know? That's how she was brought up. Even when I was young, she always kept me in tutoring programs, sports and stuff, things that would keep me away from trouble and, like, after-school programs. I worked hard, even though I was young, but still having to go to tutoring; even sometimes I hated it, but it came for a good cause because it helped me with a lot more than I was just getting for school every day. Does that make sense?

Middle School Challenges

Seventh and 8th, that's when I went to public school after going to school in the group home for a while. My aunt couldn't handle my anger and stuff, so I ended up in a group home. Rough time. Seventh grade I started back in public school. It was great. I loved middle school, man. I had great friends. Oh, I felt like I was normal, you know? I felt like I didn't have to label myself as a "group home kid" and a kid with issues.

I passed most of my classes with A's and B's. In middle school it seemed like my reading actually jumped higher because I got an opportunity to challenge myself to read bigger books. It was great for me because I love reading, and this also made my homework really easy. I got to challenge myself and I had the opportunity to read bigger books and, you know.

I'd say my favorite teacher was Ms. Danbury, my language arts teacher first period, and she was cool as heck because she would let us do journal entries at the beginning of class. I liked her because when she explained stuff, she wasn't one of those preachy teachers that was like, "I'm saying this, and you better pay attention to what I'm talking about."

No, she wasn't like that. She actually, like, took her time. You know, she wasn't one of the teachers that got irritated by your hand being raised or by questions and stuff. She didn't mind repeating herself. I could tell she was really there for the students, not just for her paycheck.

I would say science was a little bit of a problem for me in 8th grade. I wasn't doing too good in science. Math I was still passing, but science I kept flunking for some weird reason. I guess I never really understood it too much. And geography—those classes were automatic F's. People say science and math are pretty much the same thing, but I refuse to see it that way. Like with science you have these silicone shapes and you have to figure out the height and stuff. Well, really you're using math, but it's harder, and it was difficult for me. I didn't really notice math until probably middle school maybe. In middle school I just knew that I didn't like it, and I could never do it. That's when I got introduced to algebra.

My science teacher, he was cool. He assigned me to the tutor buddy, a student who could help other students and stuff after school. I ended up getting a C, which was okay, and the tutor buddy came in handy, actually, because at first I had low self-esteem with it because I was worried about being judged from being in a group home already. So I was automatically calling myself stupid. She was a nice girl and she was in 8th grade, too. And she was like, "You know, you're really cool. I know you're new here. You used to do half days, right? It's okay, I have friends that are in a group home, too. You just have to believe in yourself. I'm here to help you, you know." She gave me her number, and sometimes some of the staff there would let me call her, and we would do work over the phone. I felt normal, like I didn't have to label myself as a group home kid or a kid with issues.

Living in a group home was tough. So if I'm going through issues and, like, problems at the group home, that would affect me going to school. If I got in trouble, I wasn't allowed to go to school, which is dumb. I had to do my schoolwork at the group home.

When I was allowed to go to school they would come pick me up, the group home, in the van. It was like a regular car so sometimes I would lie and be like, "Oh, that's my dad's girlfriend," or, you know. But eventually I told the other kids, and they were really cool with it. They never judged me or nothing. You know, I still had problems and got into trouble at the group home. And my friends weren't freaked out or nothing. They felt bad, but it wasn't like a feel bad like, "Aw, you crazy bitch." It was like, "Aw, you know, we're here for you." I had great friends at that school. Great teachers, too, nice and everything. I made it through middle school.

Navigating High School

When I first started going to school when the freshman year started, that's when I realized I don't want to go to school. Too many people, I don't understand this bullshit, I don't want to try to understand this bullshit. It's not like middle school. Ooh yeah, that's when it got tricky. High school is a different ball game, you know? Sometimes you get jumped, actually beat up if you don't do this thing or that thing that they ask you to. Sometimes kids get punched so bad they're even scared to go back to school. High school, when you get to experience a lot of things. I was going to classes. I was just in some classes, but I was just, like, a careless teenager, I didn't really care about anything. I just had my own problems. Then I started skipping school a lot. Let's just say I started hanging around with the wrong crowd that were the skippers, and I skipped school a lot. I was 15, going to be 16, so in them ages you get introduced to drugs. You get introduced to partying. You get introduced to skipping school to go get high or to go have sex or whatever the case may be. So school wasn't really important to me. I'd say school wasn't as important to me anymore because I got sidetracked. Do you see what I'm saying? I didn't care for school. I feel I didn't have to go. There's this great life outside of school. I'm gonna go out and have fun.

I started getting into more trouble at the group home. They had this thing called checks, like, if I got five checks that's 5 hours in my room. So I'd get checks a lot but they stopped because it didn't matter, because I was like, "I don't care. I like being in my room." They figured kids don't mind being in their room, so then they used to lock us out of our rooms instead. Yeah, it was crazy. And that's when I started, like, running away from the group home, and then that's when I really wasn't attending school. I went to school but I didn't go to school, so let's say I would go to school in the morning and, like, leave at, like, 11:00 A.M. I got in trouble a lot of the time, but I didn't care. In 9th grade I got introduced to teenage life, so I started going to the streets. I started smoking pot, doing drugs. I didn't care about school. I really didn't care anymore about anything.

But the staff were really cool. They had a school counselor that talked to you about your problems. She understood that coming into high school, especially a freshman, can be really scary. And, you know, you might not have such a high self-esteem when it comes to wondering, "Am I gonna be able to be in high school?" She really helped. But I still flunked the 9th grade. I hated high school, honestly. I think that was one of the reasons why I dropped out, too. I don't know, I just—I bullshitted a lot of my freshman year. I'm not even gonna lie. I dropped out. I failed 9th grade, and after that I haven't been to school since.

I said to myself, "I've got freedom. I can walk off of campus. Oh, I could go smoke a cigarette. I can't do this at the group home." You know? So I guess I got introduced to the real world and fell off. I was being bad. I was just bad. This time I didn't care what anybody said. I was just doing my own thing. In the group home you don't get to experience what normal kids would do. I was just a badass. I didn't care. Like, I don't understand why I was at the group home for so long because I was like, "I'm at the age where you guys really can't tell me shit no more." I'm running away. I'm not going to school. I'm doing drugs. I'm having sex. Like I was a bad kid. My mother lost her life to the street, so I really was like, "Well fuck it, I'm not gonna be shit." My aunt evidently didn't give a fuck about me either. She put me in this group home bullshit. I was like, "Fuck life," you know?

Looking Back, Moving Forward

I don't know what I was thinking about my future or what my life would be like. No one I know that didn't graduate has ever tried to tell other kids they don't need to. In fact, all of us really regret it. We know that it really was not a good idea to stop. Honestly I thought I was gonna be like my mother. She lost her life to drugs and prostitution and that bullshit, so I really thought I would end up the same way. I really didn't care anymore about anything. I was a child when I was taken away from my life, you know, the life that I was used to. I had a lot of hate and anger, a lot of depression, a lot of, you know, suicide attempts. I was a fucked-up kid, man.

I was on the road to destruction and I knew it. And I just didn't care because when you're young you didn't think about that stuff. You think about you have all this time. Well, that time and time to do this and "I'll just do this when I feel like it." But in reality it's not like that at all. Time waits for no one.

After being on the street for a while, I tried a school program. That didn't work out, though, because too much of a bad crowd went to that program. So as you can most likely guess, it didn't work out. But then something like 5 years went by. So I was like, "The least I can do is, like, try to make something out of my life." 'Cause you know after a while when you bullshit you get tired of it 'cause it's like a repeat.

I'm finally getting somewhere. Yeah, I'm reading books again now. I passed the GED reading test. Actually I'm trying to read a lot about literature. Yeah. That's a crazy world, literature, man, I tell you. It's deep because, see, with literature you have to read between the lines. You know what I'm saying? It's not just there for you. You have to actually dig deep, you know, like Shakespeare. You know? Shakespeare didn't just put the point out there. You have to dig into it what he was saying that was greater than just what you would want to hear.

I know I need to make good choices now. Yeah, get my knowledge up. Why not? I don't be doing nothing else and, you know, I haven't done drugs in a while. 'Cause I want to be successful. You know I was always told most of my life that I wasn't gonna be anything. I was gonna end up just like my mom, you know. I refuse to be like that because I have a chance. I just have to believe in myself, and now that I am, a lot of good things are starting to happen. Slowly, but you have to start slow before you see things. You have to start somewhere, so the fact that I'm actually starting somewhere, which I never thought I'd even do, that is a lot to me.

Xavier's Story

Xavier's family background is ethnically diverse and includes Pacific Islander and European ethnicities. He feels adults stereotype him as a "gangbanger" because of his appearance. Despite some family turmoil, Xavier has always had the support of his mother and extended family members who live nearby. Xavier has an imposing frame coupled with an impassive demeanor. Anger and the need to manage his behavior have been dominant themes throughout his school life. He was suspended numerous times starting in 3rd grade and regularly skipped and failed classes all through high school.

Early School Years

Elementary—that's when I felt like I was doing the best in school. I was doing good, like, in terms of learning and grades. I was like—because yeah—I was doing good. I never really got—I don't know. I did good in, like, class-wise, but I was still getting in trouble, so . . .

I was a talkative kid then. I was always talking when I wasn't supposed to, and I had an anger management problem. The first time I got suspended was 3rd grade. I was getting bullied, and I was tired of being bullied, so I kinda hit a kid hard with a book. We both got suspended for about the same amount of time, but it was like—it was in-school suspension. It wasn't—I don't know. And the bullying didn't really stop. I just didn't like how they dealt with it. I felt they should have dealt with it more because the other kid was older. And they didn't. I didn't really think it was fair. We just got a couple days in-school suspension and no recess.

I missed a lot of recess because I was always in trouble, I guess. I wasn't very hyper, but I was talkative. I was pretty loud. And, I don't know, talking back to teachers and because I didn't like the way they talked to me, I guess. So a lot of it was for mostly talking back or being defiant.

In 4th grade I went to a new school, and it was a fresh start. I met new people. I had a new teacher I really liked, Mrs. Johnson. Her class was just a good environment. I liked her because she was equally nice to everybody, not just to one student or to a group of students. Nobody would get less punishment or get kicked out of class less often. She was really fair. She was just—I don't know—she just had a good personality. She was just a really cool teacher. She was—just one of those standout teachers.

Elementary? Yeah, I looked forward to school then. I liked seeing friends. I was able to do all the work. We did art. We were always doing stuff with papier mâché—making masks and little houses and characters from stories we'd read. I liked morning reading time—reading was always easy for me. I've always liked reading. I liked nonfiction stuff and, like, fiction, but if it was more believable, not, like, fairies and no Harry Potter stuff or nothing.

Writing was a challenge for me. Just too much stuff to remember, like punctuation . . . where a period goes, where the apostrophes go, or the commas go. It's just simple mistakes that make a huge difference in writing, and I just never remembered the punctuation. I don't know, I just didn't really like to write on boards or do group writing. Like, where we had to write on one piece of paper, when somebody was the reporter or the recorder, as they called it, just to write down. But overall I was able to do the schoolwork.

Middle School Challenges

My problems with school really started in 7th and 8th grades. Middle school kinda just got dull, you know? The teachers were not really enthused about their job. They pretty much hated their job, and when you go into a classroom, you're coming from being a kid and in a happy environment, going in middle school into a dull environment, and you can just feel the vibes the teacher gives off in the room. Most teachers I had were kinda mean in middle school.

Math has always been a challenge for me. I always knew I was a strong, good reader, but when it came to math, I wasn't as good. It wasn't that I thought I wasn't smart enough. It's just that I couldn't remember how to do a problem. When I got called on in class, I don't know, it just became a fog as I tried to remember the numbers. I knew the answer. If you asked me while I wasn't doing a test or something, I could remember. But when I was under pressure, I couldn't do it. We used to have these time sheets. One times five, two times five, you know, and they used to have this little competition where everybody was on a different times table. I got stuck on it. I was stuck on that a good six or seven months. Everybody went past me, so I knew then that math wasn't a good fit.

I never really liked to talk out loud in class, unless it was, like, talking to somebody. I didn't like the pressure of everybody looking at me, and then I would freeze up, and I would say the wrong things. People would laugh, and I didn't like feeling like that. It happened a lot. I kinda felt—I wouldn't say "dumb," I just felt embarrassed.

I hate reading out loud. Like, I will read it, you know, but sometimes, like, in my mind I can read it fine, but then when I speak out loud, it's not like when I read in my mind. So I would kind of, like, mess up and stuff. Back then, kids are going to always make fun of you about the clothes you're wearing or about whatever. They are going to say something about you. And to me, you ain't gonna say nothing about me 'cause I'm gonna punch you in the face. So it was kind of like I just tried to avoid all that.

Teachers in middle school, they weren't ever fair. . . . I got suspended a lot for fighting, being defiant, or arguing with other students. I got suspended a couple times for fighting, and I always got more time in suspension than the other kid because . . . I don't know. I wasn't the provoker. I think I was just the first one to swing or something, probably. A kid would tease me or they would poke me. Because I wasn't—I didn't get big. Everyone just thought they could pick on me. I was always letting them know I wouldn't take it. My parents knew about this because I had been talking to an anger management counselor because of what happened in 3rd grade. And for the most part, I was able to control it pretty well to how I was before. But my parents, they can't control how I act.

I think the school was always quick to suspend me, and my mom would just say, "Make him do something at school," because she had to work, so when I got sent home, I was stuck with my aunt. All I did was read when I was with my aunt. So that's why I read a lot. So I kinda didn't really mind being suspended, and my mom knew that. I just felt like I could get away with the bad behavior, I guess. I felt bad, but then again, it was like, you know, my mom's gonna be at work. I'm gonna be on my own, with no one telling me what to do. I'm not at school dealing with this bull crap with the teachers and fighting students.

I didn't skip until the end of my 8th-grade year. What classes did I start skipping? I think it was an English class . . . and then I think it was algebra class. I skipped algebra classes because . . . I can't really understand what that teacher is talking about. I skipped a half day and I thought I was gonna get in trouble. I just figured they were gonna call my house, and I wasn't gonna be able to beat my mom to the phone. But it worked out okay—I didn't get into any trouble. I didn't want to push my luck, so I only skipped a little after that.

Navigating High School

My experience in high school was mixed. For the most part teachers encouraged me to do better. They told me, "You know you can do this. You're just not putting in the effort." Or they'd say, "You're just skipping." Like they were telling me how it is. Like, yeah, they would make me wanna do better. But then in the back of my mind I was just—I felt, "I'm already so far behind, doing these assignments isn't gonna catch me up enough." For a minute I kinda lost hope, I guess I could say. There were some teachers that said, "You're gonna be another statistic. You're just going to be like everyone else who failed." Stuff like that.

Mr. Sullivan worked with me a lot. He forced me to get better at math. I don't know how he did this. He . . . he didn't talk to me like a teacher. He talked to me—he came at me like a teacher, but not like a "parent" type of teacher, "You're gonna do this my way or the highway" type thing. He was able to work with you in a way that you would understand and there's no doubt that you're not gonna understand it if he's helping you. He would go out of his way to explain, say a story problem, so that the whole class would understand it.

I didn't really like my government teacher; he was unfair. He was— he played favorites with students and was just really rude to some of us, and that would make me mad. Later on in my sophomore year, my friend had passed away. And it was really hard on a lot of us, and he— he had said something that I didn't like . . . I really didn't like. He said something disrespectful about my friend, and I just didn't go back to that class after that.

Man, I think in high school it was just a bunch of just like family stuff—and I messed up my shoulder. I had to miss school for, like, a week, I think it was, and then, we had break or whatever. And then, after I went back to school for 1 day, I finally went to the doctor. And they told me I had to get surgery. So I got the surgery and I got out. And then, I had gotten mono right after I got out, and this was right before the end of semester or quarter, or whatever. And that set me behind a lot. I also had a lot of unexcused absences because my mom had never called when we had family stuff. She did finally call, so they ended up re-enrolling me not too long after. It was, like, a couple weeks because I had to wait until I recovered from mono so I could go back to school.

I remember the principal calling me in and telling me that they get paid for me being at school, and when I'm not here they're not getting paid, so they have to withdraw me from school. After he pretty much said, "We make money off you, and we're not getting paid," I felt like, man, I didn't wanna go to school. I didn't wanna put money in his pocket. It was like me against him. He didn't really like me. We had had some bad encounters, so I'm thinking he didn't really want me back.

In 9th grade, I would skip probably a couple times a week, either mornings or afternoons. I just wouldn't skip whole days. That was never my thing. Tenth grade is kind of when I started to skip a lot toward, like—I don't know, after the first—I think it was like probably the first semester, I started skipping a lot. I started smoking weed . . . started drinking.

I had to go back to high school as a 5th-year student. I hated the environment at the school. It was just really strict. And it was just that I was older; I didn't like being treated like a kid. Sometimes I left school just because I got really mad, and I didn't wanna just end up getting suspended. So I would just leave. The security people were always on me. I couldn't have my hat on, couldn't have my headphones even showing. They, they were complaining about dress code, and, I don't know, I had bad blood with those security people because they didn't really like me. I had gotten into trouble when I was younger, and they always assumed, because of the people I hung out with, they always thought I was some gangbanger or something. They found weed in my backpack when I was a sophomore. Ever since then, if somebody got busted with pot, they always came to me, and they always searched me too. They thought I was selling weed. They would just abuse their power all the time with me, and it got to the point where it didn't even matter to me anymore. I knew I wasn't gonna get in trouble for nothing. I had nothing on me, so I'd just go and piss them off and just crack jokes at them. And I don't know, I got under their skin, so there was kinda tension between us. It wasn't working.

And so I talked to my counselor to see what I could do because my teacher, Mr. Hansen, wanted me to get my credits. And he had told me—he pretty much forced me—to talk to my counselor. He made the appointment, told me to go talk to her, so I went and talked to her. And then, he helped me write my essay to get into a credit retrieval program at the alternative school, and now I'm here. He stuck with me all the way through.

Looking Back, Moving Forward

I didn't wanna be like everyone else in my family that didn't graduate. Or who got a GED or took online classes, or whatever. I didn't wanna end up like that. None of them really were happy with a GED. My uncle and everyone else always told me I didn't have to end up like them. I didn't have to work two jobs, three jobs. If I went to school I would pretty much have it better than they had it growing up. They always told me they wished they would have stayed in school, or they wished they would have never did this, or never did that. So, I stuck it out with high school to get a diploma. "Diploma" sounds better on a job application than "GED."

After I finish, I want to work, go to a community college, and probably just get a—I don't know. I might become a drug and alcohol counselor for a little bit.

CHAPTER 4

Navigating High School

Once I got into high school, I just basically totally lost interest . . .
I didn't think school was fun, like nothing about school or no
teachers made me want to come to school. —Derrick

The beginning of high school represented a huge turning point for most
of our study participants: Although more than 90% continued into 9th
grade—a figure matching rates reported elsewhere (Taylor, 2014)—
they encountered in high school a host of new academic and social
challenges that they were poorly equipped to handle. Their high school
experiences were marred by ever-expanding academic difficulties and
accompanied by increasingly negative mindsets about their own abilities, teachers, and school in general. Serious truancy—the frequent,
persistent, and deliberate skipping of classes—became the norm for this
group.

The chapter begins with a look at increased academic struggles
youth participants faced in high school and their accompanying mindsets and behaviors. We then turn to peer-related issues that figured cen-
trally in their experience of school at this stage. Finally, we examine
truant behavior in the high school context and its serious consequences.

INCREASED ACADEMIC STRUGGLES

As we saw in earlier chapters, most participants showed signs of academic struggles and disengagement years before dropping out. In high
school, multiple learning-related factors became more prominent and
deleterious as the academic stakes increased, contributing to a process
of increased disengagement. These factors included:

- Insufficient skills and behaviors necessary for academic success
- Insufficient academic support
- Fixed mindsets that undermined motivation and effort

- Negative perceptions of classroom and school climate
- Lack of engaging, student-centered learning

Academic Challenges, Negative Mindsets

The majority of youth participants encountered academic difficulties in middle school that were not fully addressed. As a result, most participants entered high school ill-prepared to meet the new and greater academic demands placed on them, further deepening their detrimental beliefs about their abilities. Many vividly recalled feeling overwhelmed almost immediately by the new demands:

> And then . . . I started not understanding the work . . . so I started falling behind and stuff; that's when I started not liking school. People were like, "Oh, high school will be better," but I got into high school and it was even worse. —Derrick

Even students like Xavier and Callie, who had passed all their classes in middle school, now encountered serious academic problems, including course failure, and began to doubt they could make it through. Here are Xavier's thoughts about finishing 10th grade:

> But then in the back of my mind I was just—I felt, "I'm already so far behind, doing these assignments isn't gonna catch me up enough." For a minute I kinda lost hope, I guess I could say. —Xavier

Beliefs About Teachers. Participants believed that once they had earned the reputation of being poor students, they were stuck in that role. Derrick, for example, was convinced that his high school teachers preferred to help the more capable students, not struggling students like him:

> So I felt like the star students in high school got engaged more by the teachers, and all the kids like me, you know, we sometimes show up late or goof around in class. I just wouldn't get the help that I needed. . . . The star students could get help in class, but the teachers made all the kids that are bad come in after school. —Derrick

The perception that teachers could not or would not help those who most needed it, shared by Trisha and many other participants facing learning challenges, reflected a deeply pessimistic view not only of their teachers, but also of their academic identities. They were the "bad" students, the ones that the teachers in some sense had rejected in favor of the good students. These negative perceptions of teachers and of self further contributed to a downward academic spiral, leading to course failure. Unlike in middle grades, however, course failure in high school had far-reaching negative consequences for graduation (and beyond).

Academic Struggles, Mindset, and Behavior. Struggling students' constant academic setbacks in high school, negative perceptions of teachers, and fixed mindsets regarding their own abilities heightened their disaffection for school. These factors help explain why participants' overall enjoyment of school plummeted in high school, while truancy increased. In middle school, a majority of participants (59%) still viewed school positively; by early high school, this number dwindled to just 22% (see Figure 2.1).

Derrick's recounting of his high school academic experiences exemplified the pernicious effects that unresolved learning challenges can have on student mindset and, subsequently, on attendance. Derrick wasted no time deciding he could never learn high school Spanish; rather than taking time to study or ask for help, he simply gave up after the first week of class:

> One class I remember skipping a lot was Spanish class. At first I was like, "Yeah, I get to learn Spanish." And then the first week went through and I was like, "I can't do this. This is horrible." And so I just, like, never went to that class. —Derrick

Classroom Conflict. For some, like Derrick and Xavier, negative learning situations in high school gave rise to conflicts in class. Frustration led to angry exchanges with a teacher or an administrator, which in turn led to a negative counter-response from the adult and a further escalation of the conflict. This scenario often terminated in a disciplinary response from the school and/or in the student walking away upset. For Xavier, the perception that teachers were unfair or disrespectful frequently triggered his anger. When asked about the kinds of things that got him mad in class, he gave this example:

> I didn't really like my government teacher . . . my friend had passed away. And it was really hard on a lot of us, and he . . . said something disrespectful about my friend, and I just didn't go back to that class after that. —Xavier

In contrast, Derrick believed his anger problems stemmed from a sense of being abandoned. He felt trapped in a system in which he now believed he could not succeed. When Derrick pleaded for help and did not receive it immediately in class, his frustration would get the better of him. He drew a direct line between his academic situation, the teacher's perceived indifference, and his angry response, which led to skipping:

> So I'd sit there like, "I don't know how to do this," and the teachers would be like, "Well, we went over it." . . . I'd get mad, and teachers would tell me, "You can go to the office." "I'm not going to the office. I'm going to go off campus and go find something to do until the class is over.". . . That's where the skipping thing started. —Derrick

For both Derrick and Xavier, negative interactions with school personnel fed a propensity to withdraw effort, skip classes, and fail. Their accounts of behavior problems in high school highlighted an unproductive interplay between students and the adults in charge of their learning. The final chapter will explore ways that this dynamic might be disrupted.

Problems with One-Size-Fits-All Instruction

As discussed in Chapter 3, a one-size-fits-all instructional approach, especially in mathematics, discouraged engagement and persistence in middle school. When struggling students encountered similar learning contexts in high school, they fell further behind and saw no way forward. Individualized support that was largely present in elementary grades, and less available in middle school, all but vanished by the beginning of high school, which is when Derrick, Trisha, Yolanda, and other struggling students started to disappear from classrooms.

In high school, homework became an increasingly important aspect of the one-size-fits-all curriculum; youth participants' sporadic completion of assignments had been an ongoing problem since middle school, but now led to academic disaster, especially in math. In addition, a new homework-related theme became more salient: Students' inability to do the assigned work independently. They did not understand lessons fully enough to be able to successfully apply their partial understanding to subsequent homework assignments:

> I think it was the homework part too . . . and then having to bring it back in. By the time I got home and I was ready to do my homework,

that class period was already fading away, and I was forgetting how to do things. —Callie

For these students, homework did not fulfill the purpose of practicing newly learned academic and self-regulatory skills (National Mathematics Advisory Panel, 2008). Moreover, as Chapter 5 discusses, many did not have ready access to parental assistance or other resources to support homework practice and completion. These findings resonate with research suggesting that math homework, in particular, actually may *decrease* self-efficacy and achievement for students who need extra help, but who have more limited access to support resources, like parental assistance (Kitsantas, Cheema, & Ware, 2011). Frustration over homework impeded youths' ability to keep up with subjects and further contributed to the cycle of negative attitudes toward learning, withdrawal of effort, avoidance through truancy, and academic failure.

As was the case with their narratives about middle school, almost no participants could recall an enjoyable or interesting learning activity during high school. Callie was one of the few who remembered a meaningful assignment, one that substantially departed from a one-size-fits-all approach for a history lesson:

> And my teacher, he finally—he comes out with this project . . . we pretend that we are a person in that time. And we have to do a journal with a map. . . . I got all excited, and so I went and got, like, a leather notebook thing. I made sure I used, like, a fancy pen . . . and I got to use my creative writing skills. But I also had to do the research for it. —Callie

Even though the activity was for a subject she normally did not like, it made a lasting impression on her because it contained multiple ingredients supporting student engagement: acknowledgment of student interests, room for creative expression, and hands-on demonstration of skills and knowledge guided by student choice.

Reading Challenges in High School

Reading emerged as an area of academic challenge for youth participants in their high school years, as evidenced in both the reading experiences they could recall and those they could *not* recall, despite multiple interview questions and follow-up prompts. As described in Chapter 2, most considered themselves to be competent readers in their elementary years, but by the middle grades this confidence waned; their narratives reflected a downward trend from "I'm a good reader" to "reading got boring," which continued into high school.

"I'm a Good Reader." Many participants, including Yolanda, considered themselves "good readers" as young children, a positive view explained in part by the phases of early reading development in which reading is primarily a task of decoding words that are already part of a reader's oral language vocabulary (Ehri, 1995):

> I've always liked reading. That was my thing. Reading was easy for me. Man, it was really easy. I guess when I was young I really was always reading. —Yolanda

This sense of reading confidence in early years can decline as children move up through the elementary grades (McKenna et al., 1995) and the demands of reading shift from decoding to comprehending increasingly challenging texts (Brown, 2002). This shift presented considerable challenges to youth participants; although some maintained that they were good readers, others acknowledged increasing struggles comprehending assigned readings across multiple subject areas.

"Reading Got Boring." Beginning in middle school, and accelerating into high school, reading demands become increasingly complex as textbooks replace stories, picture books, and accessible texts:

> Reading was difficult most of the time, but sometimes not. It depended on the grade-level book I was reading. . . . I struggled with that, especially without the extra help like I got in elementary school. —Trisha

Youth participants often saw textbooks as boring; few could recall anything they read in high school, assigned or chosen. Even Jack, who recalled reading Shakespeare in high school, could not remember anything else he had read. This striking absence of reading memories leads us to suspect many struggled with reading during high school but did not want to reveal this shortcoming: Not being good at reading appeared shameful to admit. Rather than being "good readers who got bored," it was likely that reading assignments, especially from textbooks, were too difficult. Participants like Derrick and Trisha who were struggling readers in elementary or middle school were not prepared for reading these complex texts, despite having previously received support services.

Faced with assignments they couldn't finish and books they couldn't comprehend, reading motivation and engagement declined.

We know that adolescent motivation to read may be impacted by perceived difficulty, feelings of incompetence, and the perception of reading as useless (Guthrie, Klauda, & Ho, 2013). It would seem that these factors coalesced to discourage youths from reading or even trying to read in high school classes.

Instructional Approaches to Reading. Rather than providing reading instruction, high school teachers appeared to assign readings and require students to answer questions about the readings in class. Such academic tasks have been shown to negatively impact student motivation (Legault, Green-Demers, & Pelletier, 2006). Further, students were asked to take turns reading aloud. Youth participants who mentioned this practice of "round-robin reading" loathed it, seeing it as a source of peer humiliation:

> I hate reading out loud. Like, I will read it, you know, but sometimes, like, in my mind I can read it fine, but then when I speak out loud, it's not like when I read in my mind. So I would kind of, like, mess up and stuff. —Xavier

While participants recalled teachers lecturing and having students take turns reading out loud, none mentioned the use of discussion or conversation as a way to foster engaged reading. This reported lack of classroom talk is surprising, given the growing body of research showing how classroom talk leads to engaged reading and benefits learning (Almasi, McKeown, & Beck, 1996).

Frustrated by challenging texts and determined to avoid boring assignments and humiliating activities, students became disengaged readers and looked for a way out. Both a decrease in reading motivation and negative identities as readers contributed to further disengagement from school and skipping behaviors.

The Math Tripwire Revisited

As described in Chapter 3, middle school math emerged as a serious academic tripwire over which the majority of participants stumbled and never recovered. In high school these math difficulties intensified. Many who had struggled in pre-algebra classes were now trying to cope with the advanced math required for graduation.

"I'm No Good in Math." An important concept related to mindset is *self-efficacy*, which concerns an individual's perceptions of his/her ability

to learn and perform in a particular area (Bandura, 1997). Many participants consistently expressed low self-efficacy in math in high school, even those who did not indicate struggling with math in earlier grades:

> I think my problems really started with math. I just didn't get it.
> Probably math class was the most challenging one for me. That's where I started disliking school because the teacher didn't help out as much as I'd wanted. —Derrick

Algebra continued to pose significant problems for students who were challenged by its abstract nature and questioned the relevance of the subject to their lives. Many recalled failing algebra and having to repeat the class—but never managing to pass.

A Math Gender Gap. A larger portion of participants associated serious learning difficulties with math (68%) than with reading (51%). However, reported learning problems in math were not equally distributed across male and female participants. Gender comparisons reveal that fully 90% of female participants described having serious problems with math. In comparison, only 55% of male participants discussed serious math issues. While there may be many reasons for this discrepancy, research suggests gender differences in math may be due in large part to girls' sense of lower self-efficacy rather than ability (Kitsantas et al., 2011).

Instructional Approaches to Mathematics. Participants did not fare well with the lecture-style approach commonly used in high school math classes. There was no guided practice or group work, just "I do" (the teacher demonstrating a concept or method) and "you do" (students then asked to apply what the teacher demonstrated). Students interpreted this instructional approach to mean that they should "get it" the first time around, and that if they did not understand, they were largely on their own:

> Whatever we're learning in math, they teach it once and then you just have to, like, do it by yourself or figure it out, how to do it on your own, right? So, I didn't like that. —Callie

Being left to figure it out on their own further frustrated and demotivated youths. More than any other subject, math was connected to academic problems, skipping class, and serious truancy by high school. In the final chapter we consider the question, "What might schools do differently to prevent an I'm-no-good-in-math mindset from taking hold?"

PEER ISSUES IN HIGH SCHOOL

Now we turn to peer-related issues that seemed to greatly impact youth participants' experiences in high school: difficult social transitions and bullying. These issues surfaced in middle school as well, but they often became most consequential for participants during high school.

Social Transitions and Transfer Woes

In addition to academic struggles in high school, participants faced challenging social adjustments. They described the painful loss of friendships in high school as social groupings shifted over time, when those they thought were friends pulled away. They talked about not fitting in, not getting along, or not understanding why they were being rejected. For academically overwhelmed students like Derrick, this sudden social loss magnified the misery of being in school, providing another reason for being truant:

> Everyone changes in high school and stuff. They find, like, who they really want to kick it with. . . . I just didn't really like that change. . . . There's some friends that I don't even talk to anymore. —Derrick

Being socially and academically adrift, Derrick eventually joined a new peer group of similarly alienated students. In the next chapter, we describe the many negative influences such a peer group can have on already vulnerable youths.

Social transition issues were most apparent in conjunction with *student mobility*. Often participants attended five or more schools from kindergarten through early high school, due to family disruption, housing instability, or problems at school. Multiple school transfers are a strong predictor of dropping out (Rumberger, 2011). Students in foster care, for example, have among the lowest graduation rates of any group, due in part to the multiple placements and resulting school transfers that they commonly experience (Legal Center for Foster Care & Education, 2014).

Interestingly, few interviewees characterized school transfers that occurred at the elementary level as problematic for them. At that stage, some even found the change exciting, providing them with a fresh start. For older students, however, the transition to a new learning environment was often unsettling and socially difficult, especially if external forces, such as family reconfiguration, economic loss, or expulsion, compelled the move. Thus, transfers during high school seemed particularly difficult for participants. Their narratives help explain some of the mechanisms underlying the widely recognized correlation cited earlier between school transfers and negative school outcomes. Here are several scenarios participants recalled in transitioning to a new high school.

"Feelings of Isolation and Alienation Overwhelmed Me." Students felt cut off from established friendships and could not always make new friends quickly or easily, especially in late middle and high school, where social interactions were typically more constrained by solidified peer groups (Zimmer-Gembeck & Collins, 2003). Participants described painful social experiences associated with transferring to a new school—sitting alone during lunchtime, having no friends, and feeling lost or even intimidated by a new and unfamiliar school setting:

> I transferred to alternative school, but I was just—I kind of kept to myself. I wasn't really used to the new school. It was like being an outcast, really. —Trisha

In line with research findings on emotional stress and adolescent learning (Tough, 2016), this subgroup of participants reported that painful emotions associated with a transfer so dominated their school experiences that they had difficulty focusing on academic work.

"I Couldn't Turn to Peers or Teachers for Support." Transfer students lacked important peer supports such as a study partner, a friend to turn to for advice or support, or someone to call for information about a missed assignment. Without these supports they felt vulnerable and were particularly sensitive to being judged, not only by peers from whom they were seeking acceptance, but also by teachers, with whom they had no personal history. As a new transfer student, for example, Trisha recalled she could not bring herself to ask for much-needed help in math class:

> I would never raise my hand to ask a question. Probably because I was feeling shy. And then the other thing is that, I don't know . . . it probably was because I didn't have any friends in class. So I was just, like, embarrassed, or something like that. —Trisha

"I Was Ambushed by Shifting Academic Expectations." Transfer students felt negatively impacted by a perceived lack of academic continuity. In their previous school, they might not have covered the material or learned concepts and skills they were now expected to know. For already struggling students, this set of circumstances was particularly damaging: They could not understand or catch up; their daily experiences confirmed they were not successful students.

"I Joined Other Alienated Peers." As we have already seen, academic struggles often seemed to trigger skipping behaviors. Similarly, we found that socially isolated transfer students, in their quest to belong, drifted toward peers who also felt alienated, who were in a skipping culture, and who were likely to encourage a newcomer like Trisha to join in:

> Yeah. I was around a whole bunch of kids that were skipping, so at the time, you know, it seems like you should, too. It's hard finding who to hang around with and who not to, I guess. Because at the time you just kind of want to be accepted. —Trisha

Bullying and Aggression at School

School-based bullying is a serious problem, negatively affecting the health, well-being, and academic performance of up to 30% of all school-aged children in the United States (National Academies of Sciences, Engineering, and Medicine, 2016). At least one quarter of the youths we interviewed experienced bullying or threats of violence that negatively impacted their school experience. Bullying at any stage was harmful, but the connection between bullying, truancy, and school failure was especially clear during high school. Even when students themselves were not the victims of bullying or violence, the potential for being victimized unsettled them:

> High school is a different ball game, you know? Sometimes you get jumped, actually beat up if you don't do this thing or that thing that they ask you to. Sometimes kids get punched so bad they're even scared to go back to school. —Yolanda

Yolanda never admitted to being the one who was "jumped" or "scared to go back," but her truant behavior commenced right around the same time that she experienced (or witnessed) these aggressions at her new school.

In many participants' accounts, the connection between feeling unsafe and attendance was explicit; the student embraced an avoidance strategy, making a conscious decision to spend time away from school. Victims typically felt that schools could not or would not protect them:

> The school was totally aware of what had been happening. I'd been going and telling the principal, telling my counselor—all these people— telling so many people that I was constantly being picked on. —Jack

For students like Jack, Trisha, and Yolanda, this sense that school authorities had been unjust or uninterested in their plight acted as a wedge, further alienating already vulnerable students from school and spurring decisions to skip class more often.

SERIOUS TRUANCY

As discussed in Chapter 3, parental and school interventions proved ineffective in curtailing the sporadic and experimental skipping that, for many youth participants, began in middle school. By the end of 9th grade or early 10th grade, virtually all had advanced to the third phase in the dropping out process, which is characterized by more serious truancy. They reported skipping classes regularly in high school, often missing half or whole days of school at a time:

> In 9th grade, I would skip probably a couple times a week, either mornings or afternoons. I just wouldn't skip whole days. That was never my thing. Tenth grade is kind of when I started to skip a lot. —Xavier

Within this more advanced phase of truancy, participants tended to fall into two groups: those who skipped certain classes on a regular basis and those who routinely missed whole days (or nearly whole days) of school. Participants like Xavier presented their decision to skip only certain days and times as a conscious choice, always keeping one foot in the action at school and only skipping and failing certain classes. They tended to be "slow faders," whose dropping out process extended over years. Participants like Yolanda, in contrast, started to engage in more wholesale skipping, putting themselves on a faster track to academic failure and dropping out.

Whatever the pattern, ongoing truant behavior became a central and consequential feature of students' pathways to dropping out: The more school they missed, the more courses they failed, falling further and further behind in credits needed to graduate. The next chapter explores how peer groups can encourage struggling students to embrace truancy, despite its obvious negative consequences.

CONCLUSION

For the majority of participants, high school represented not only a transition, but also a continuation of a dynamic process involving academic failure, progressive disengagement, and withdrawal of effort from school. The origins of this narrative often stretched back to early middle school and sometimes even elementary grades. Many of the same components of disengagement described in the previous chapter—unaddressed learning issues, poor academic habits, alienation from teachers and subject matter, and negative mindsets—figured prominently in youths' stories about high school. However, students' behaviors, attitudes, and beliefs had had more time to solidify around the notion that they did not belong in school. Additionally, nonacademic issues associated with student transitions and bullying became more salient at this stage.

Developmentally, youth participants had moved from early to middle or later adolescence, a period typically marked by the waning of adult influence and the adolescent's increased desire for greater autonomy and independent decisionmaking (Zimmer-Gembeck & Collins, 2003). As these older adolescents became more and more alienated from school, a place many saw as unwelcoming or unsafe, they increasingly sought to feel more competent and more in control of their lives by disobeying authority and avoiding school on a regular basis. The increase in truant behavior during high school had dire consequences: It led to course failures that imperiled their chances for graduation.

This developmental trajectory has serious implications for dropout prevention: The older the adolescents and the more firmly entrenched their beliefs about school and their own abilities, the harder it becomes to intervene. Although they may not have realized it at the time, once participants chose serious truancy as their solution to school problems, they had crossed a Rubicon of sorts: They continued on a pathway that inevitably led to dropping out. Chapter 6 examines interviewees' motivations and decisionmaking around the final step of leaving school and their divergent paths after dropping out. Before moving to participants' exits from school, however, we turn in Chapter 5 to an important theme not yet discussed: the role of personal and family issues in influencing the dropping out process.

Trisha's Story

Trisha's positive demeanor, toothy smile, and cascade of dark curly hair suggest confidence and maturity beyond her years. Growing up African American in a small and almost entirely White community wasn't easy for her; she was often bullied and excluded. Trisha attributed her school problems to racial tension, which, along with her parents separating when she was in middle school, led to anger issues, fights with other students, and academic decline. In addition, she struggled with learning issues, particularly in reading, that she felt set her further apart from her peers. By early high school, Trisha was in a precarious situation and at risk of academic failure.

Early School Years

I always hated school. Well, preschool wasn't so bad because we got to play most of the time. It was more once I got into elementary school—1st grade and on. I liked the whole idea of learning, but I didn't like that somebody that I didn't really know was bossing me around. School was never really for me. I got held back in 1st grade. I had a hard time learning to read, and they—they said that they wanted to make sure that I got down all of the basic skills that every other 1st-grader had because they didn't feel like I did, so that's why they held me back. I had a lot of help in elementary—I don't know how to explain it. It was like I needed a push sometimes. I remember when I was younger I just didn't think I was good in math. I just didn't think I could do it, you know? Like, I'd be on one math question, and I'd be like, "Okay, I have half of it figured out, but I can't think of the rest." Then, I'd have the teacher there, but—yeah.

I liked reading, but in elementary school, it was definitely more difficult back then for me. But they put me in—I don't know what they called the classes—special education. But a lot of kids I went to school with were in those classes, too, so it wasn't like—nobody made fun of anybody for that. Those classes eventually got me on the right track, and I got a little bit ahead in reading. Then, from, like, 5th grade on, I was ahead in reading, and it wasn't so hard anymore.

I made lots of good friends in elementary school, but I had to leave them behind when I moved here. It was hard because we moved, and I ended up going to three or four different schools. I did go to one school where there weren't so many other African Americans like me, so it was—I felt a lot of the time like I was discriminated against. I definitely got discriminated against on my soccer team and stuff when I was little, but that's part of the reason why we moved away from there because I was the only African American in my grade. My parents wanted to make sure that I didn't have to feel that way—that I was the only kid like me.

Mrs. Jameson, she wasn't like any other teacher I've ever met. She, like, genuinely, like, actually cared. We had a classroom pet; it was a hamster. She let me take him home for summer break, and she ended up not having room in her new classroom, so she let me keep him. We eventually ended up giving him to my aunt's parents because we ran out of room, so we had to move him in with them. But—3rd grade was definitely—Mrs. Jameson was my favorite teacher.

In 5th grade we went on a field trip to the state capitol. We went in all of the buildings, and I thought it was cool because our school rented, like, the really nice buses and took all the 5th-grade classes there, so my favorite part was at the end of the year when we got to go on our big field trip.

Middle School Challenges

Middle school was hard because you go from a really different environment, from an elementary to a middle school, and the kids there are pretty mean, so getting used to that takes a while, I guess, and that distracts you from what else is going on and you need to take care of. I had one special reading class for a term, and that was it. They decided that they didn't want to keep me in those classes, even though I definitely didn't feel like I was ready to not be in those classes. I think, like, my schoolwork kind of suffered from that. My grades were really good in elementary school, but I'm sure if anyone looked at my grades from then on into middle school you'd see that, once they took me out of those classes, my grades went down. So it's like, in elementary I was doing really well. Then, middle school on, not so good. When I got into 7th grade, it was—it was a challenge, but it wasn't too hard. In 8th grade, it was harder. Then, in high school, it got harder and harder.

Reading was difficult most of the time, but sometimes not. It depended on the grade-level book I was reading. Yeah, but it was usually hard, especially when what they do is give everyone a copy of the book, and then somebody reads a section and somebody else reads a section, so we're all reading out loud. I struggled with that, especially without the extra help, like I got in elementary school. Writing was always easy. It just came to me. Since I can remember, writing has always come to me. I paid extra attention in history because that was one of my favorites and I liked writing. That was about it. I failed classes in math. In 8th grade it was pre-algebra, but it was just because I wasn't doing my homework and turning it in because I didn't want to. I don't know why. I just didn't. I didn't really like homework in general. It wasn't like I was a rebellious kid or anything. Yeah—I never turned in my work when I was in elementary school. No one was home to help me, so when I didn't understand something or didn't have supplies around to do a project, I just didn't do the assignments. I just followed the same pattern in middle and high school, but then I failed because of it.

It seemed like the middle school had way more students, like, at least two times the students than the school could even accommodate, so every classroom was packed full of kids. Honestly, I don't think the teachers really had expectations for anybody other than students that were special to them because there were so many of us that I don't think that they put expectations on each and every one of us. I just felt like they wouldn't have enough time to get to me, let alone everybody else, or even know who we were.

In middle school I was more concentrated on trying to figure out why my dad left. I feel like I was really a confused kid at that point, with my biological dad not being around, so I was more preoccupied with that kind of stuff than I was with school. Also, the bullying started. Once I got into the 6th grade in middle school, there was only one other African American kid, so it was difficult. I could just brush it off then, but when it was a lot of kids continuing to do it, it got to me. I felt discriminated against by other kids. These girls would call me racial slurs, and they'd poke at me and poke at me. Then it ended up getting physical—four girls jumped me a couple times actually—in 8th grade and then in 10th grade. They kind of just really didn't give up bullying me until I left for good.

The school didn't really do anything about the bullying other than suspending us all for a couple days. They told me that they really couldn't do anything without evidence from a teacher, and girls are sneaky. I was actually friends with those girls for a long time, and I don't know what happened. All of a sudden they just didn't like me, and after that is when they started bullying. My parents tried to work with the school, but the school didn't really help. So we eventually had to just move schools.

Navigating High School

When 9th grade started, I was doing well. Then, a couple terms in I started getting F's and D's. Then, after that, I just didn't even want to try because I felt like it was too much work to get all my grades up. I mean I didn't really care about school. I would never raise my hand to ask a question. Probably because I was feeling shy. And then the other thing is that, I don't know . . . it probably was because I didn't have any friends in class. So I was just, like, embarrassed or something like that. I just wanted to hang out with the friends that I did have and do whatever I wanted. I was—I did rebel in high school, but I don't know why I really—I just didn't like going to school. A couple times a week I'd just skip to be with friends. We'd just hang out, go around town.

The school didn't really do anything. They didn't seem like they cared that much because there's so many kids that go to one school. I don't feel like they feel a need to, like, care about every single student other than what they have to do.

I don't think my parents really knew what to do because I was their only child, and this was the first time that they were going through this. I think they kind of tiptoed and tried not to push me. I was never grounded or anything like that. I don't think they wanted to push me too hard to the point where I wanted to run away or something along those lines. They were disappointed, but my mom said, "You're going to have to learn on your own what you want and what you don't; I'm not going to force you to go to school, because it will hit you when it hits you." And, it definitely did.

In the 10th grade I kept getting bullied. Finally two girls picked a fight with me. They all jumped on me, and we got pulled apart. I got suspended I think longer than them—because I don't think they wanted me to come back to school when they came back because they were scared it was gonna cause another problem. I didn't go back. I tried alternative school instead.

I transferred to alternative school, but I was just—I kind of kept to myself. I wasn't really used to the new school. It was like being an outcast, really. But one teacher there was so nice. Sandra always told me, "You're a leader. You are beautiful. You're a good person. Don't let what anybody says bring you down." Stuff like that. I had more of a close relationship with Sandra than any of the other teachers there. It was good at first. I was getting good grades, and then, well—they're too lenient, so then, that made it easier to skip because they were right in the middle of town. Yeah. I was around a whole bunch of kids that were skipping, so at the time, you know, it seems like you should, too. It's hard finding who to hang around with and who not to, I guess. Because at the time you just kind of want to be accepted. They let you leave school for lunch, so I would just not go back after lunch. I would go and hang out with my friends and just do whatever—I don't even know.

I was 17, almost 18—like, 6 months until I was 18—when the court got involved. A month before I turned 18, they let me off because I was going to be 18, and they couldn't do anything. I just ended it with the alternative school after I turned 18—just not really going anymore. What was the point? I would stay at home and sleep all day.

Looking Back, Moving Forward

I just think I was really immature. I just shouldn't have been able to make my own decisions—because I always made bad ones. I didn't like when my parents said they were disappointed in me, and they'd play that card a lot. They tried to do whatever they could to get me to go to school, but I just wouldn't comply. They definitely weren't happy about my choices, but once I grew up a little and figured out that my GED or my high school diploma was really something that I really needed to have, they pushed me and helped me get it. I just think I struggled with a lot of personal problems throughout school. I was too distracted to study or learn. I feel like that's mostly the reason why I didn't really have an interest in school and stopped trying. If I could go back now, I would do things differently. It was just because I think with everything going on I just kind of mixed up my priorities, I didn't have them straight. I had a lack of focus because of everything going on around school and my life at that point.

I think maybe my parents could have been more strict, but I don't know what to think about schools. Just a lot of them seem like they don't take an interest in a lot of kids that I've seen. Because there are a lot of kids that had similar problems like me, and they didn't really seem to care either about that.

Later I knew I was going get my GED, because at that point I had grown up a little bit and realized that I needed to do something. And I was dead set on getting my GED, and I did. Next I want to go to college for early childhood education and be a preschool teacher. That's my plan so far.

Derrick's Story

Derrick is a Caucasian young man who closely identifies with hip-hop culture. Short and stocky, he sports a backwards baseball cap and baggy jeans. Derrick seems alternately anguished and angry whenever he reflects on his urban middle school and high school experiences. Because of his significant reading problems, school was never easy for Derrick, but he still managed to enjoy his elementary years. However, almost from the moment he entered middle school, he struggled to deal with academic and social demands placed on him. He clowned around, got into trouble, and regularly failed classes. By 8th grade he was well on a pathway to dropping out.

Early School Years

My earliest memories of school were in kindergarten. I remember we had learning stations with different activities, and I really liked that. All of the activities were cool. I don't remember every station, but I remember there were, like, the big building blocks, the big cardboard building blocks.

I liked elementary school the most, probably because I was little, and it was, like, going to school, you know, it's fresh then. You like it a lot—but then, some kids don't like it. There was those times when I didn't want to get up and go to school, but in elementary school, I felt like there was always something fun to do there, and it was fun learning and stuff, and the teachers were nice, and all that. And then you had, like, your one class all year. The thing that I kind of mostly remember is music class and recess—those were the things that I liked, so . . . But, like, the rest, like, reading and math class, not really.

I don't think I, like, wanted to read in elementary school. I didn't want to read anything that much. I don't remember many books I read. I wasn't a very good reader. That's probably why I wasn't interested. Like, in elementary school they made all the kids go into a reading class at the start of the day and there's different levels of reading and all that. And I was always in the low levels, like, not a very good reader. And then I got into middle school, and they put me into the special reading class.

Middle School Challenges

Once I got into middle school, I picked up a few books and read them by myself. I don't know why. I probably just found the right books that I liked, the right series. So I read a few of those. And then I read some big books, too, through high school, but I don't really read much. I didn't really read any books or even remember nothing. I didn't have time for it. Stuff was happening so I didn't really have patience to sit down and read.

They put me into this special reading program. So I was in there for, like, half of 7th grade all the way until, like, the end of 9th grade. Finally they graduated me out of the reading class and said I was a good reader. I thought that reading class was really boring. I'm not saying it was bad, I just don't understand why I needed it.

I always liked 7th-grade science because we did hands-on activities. We used the microscopes and all that, and we were able to put slides together. I remember one time in science we got to dissect a frog to learn about organs. And then we put some tissue under the microscope, and I thought that was pretty cool. We did a lot of hands-on stuff that I liked in science. But I don't like sitting and reading out of books.

I think my problems really started with math. I just didn't get it. Probably math class was the most challenging one for me. That's where

I started disliking school because the teacher didn't help out as much as I'd wanted. In middle school, we had this one math teacher, and he was really good, and I liked him, but then he ended up having to move, so we got this new math teacher, and I didn't like her at all. Like, she didn't even teach us. She'd give us a worksheet, and she'd tell us about the worksheet, and we'd sit there the whole class, and she would maybe help us a little bit. We all ended up passing the class, only because she gave us the answers the whole year.

I think I was one of the kids that was still being a kid, so I wasn't acting my age yet. Once you hit middle school, that's when it's like you're not in elementary any more. You're not a little kid, you're more of a— you're still a little kid, but you're kind of at that age when you wanna do what you wanna do. And so that's why I think I kind of went down.

In my middle school, we had this thing called Positive Action. If you'd get in trouble in the middle of the class, you'd get a write-up, you know, and then they'd send you to a special room. I went to this room a lot. I was there probably every other day. I was being a class clown and just having fun, but the teachers wouldn't like it, and they'd say, "Stop." And I'd control myself for a while, but then it would just start again, and the teacher would say, "Okay, you've got to leave."

I remember they would have all-day detention in middle school. I had that a few times. We'd go and we'd sit there all day in the class. I'd have to stay in a little room at lunch, you know, so I wouldn't be able to skip during lunch. And I was happy to be with my friend, so I don't know why the school would do that. Like, it was kinda dumb because my friend was there, so I wouldn't care if I was there. Sometimes that was fun. It just depended on who was in the detention room that day.

I liked coming to middle school at the start, having all the new people there instead of the same ones I'd been with for the whole 6 years in elementary school and all that. And then some of the teachers and me just didn't get along good. I didn't understand the work, and I couldn't get all the help that I needed, and that's when I started not liking school. The class sizes were all big. There were maybe 30 kids in most of them.

And then I started not understanding the work. I wouldn't be using anything I learned in school out in everyday life. Like advanced math and geometry and all that. It's not like I'm going to be a rocket scientist. So I started falling behind and stuff; that's when I started not liking school. People were like, "Oh, high school will be better," but I got into high school and it was even worse.

Navigating High School

Once I got into high school, I just basically totally lost interest. I don't know what I was thinking. I guess I was a late bloomer. I always wanted to be a kid. And then finally, I think it was when I hit high school, I was finally like, "Oh, I need to grow up." I knew I could do the work. I just wasn't committed to it. There was nothing pushing me to do it. Some people are like, "Oh, yeah, I do all the work 'cause I want to get into a good college." Or, "I want to make my parents happy." I was just, like, blah about it. I can't say I really know why. I was just never fond of school. I felt like it never got along with me either.

Everyone changes in high school and stuff. They find, like, who they really want to kick it with, and who they really want to be and all that. . . . I just didn't really like that change. . . . There's some friends that I don't even talk to anymore. It'd be nice to talk to them 'cause I liked them back then, but going into high school they started changing, and it's like, "I don't like you that much anymore." I didn't think school was fun, like nothing about school or no teachers made me want to come to school. You know how everyone usually has that teacher that they are just like, "Oh, yeah, they make me want to come to school." I didn't really have that. I didn't feel like I had any teachers that I liked enough to get up and go see every day and let them know, "Hey, I'm here, I'm okay." Plus, there's also, like, the "star" students at high school. So I felt like the star students in high school got engaged more by the teachers, and all the kids like me, you know, we sometimes show up late or goof around in class. I just wouldn't get the help that I needed. It was just moving too fast for me. I'm not a fast learner. So I felt like I was . . . like all the kids that didn't do well or anything, we were getting singled out. The star students could get help in class, but the teachers made all the kids that are bad come in after school or go in on their time. I didn't think it was fair. We're in class to learn, so we should all have an equal opportunity to ask questions and all that.

Then when I started with new math classes where teachers are rougher, I'm like, "I don't know any of this," so they would make me come in after school or on my time. I'd get the occasional student that would help out, you know, the nice student, rather than the teacher. I felt the math teachers didn't help me as best as they could. I wasn't a fast learner. I needed a little extra time. And with class sizes being so big in high school and all that, it's just everything was moving so quick. So I'd sit there like, "I don't know how to do this," and the teachers would be like, "Well, we went over it." It's like, "I just need a little extra help. You can't give it to me?" And then the teachers would be like, "Oh, well, you should be able to do better." And so that's where they get mixed up. People think they know who we are, but they really don't!

I'd get mad, and teachers would tell me, "You can go to the office." "I'm not going to the office. I'm going to go off campus and go find something to do until the class is over." Or something like that. I'd just get frustrated and I'd leave. That's where the skipping thing started. They would kick me out and be like, "Go to the office." So I would just get frustrated and I'd leave. And I would just find a friend or something like that that's ready to leave and be like, "Okay, let's go."

The work just started getting hard and I just didn't understand and all that. So I was just like, "I can't do this, so I'm not going to waste my time coming in and sitting here and feeling dumb the whole time." I never did homework or anything. Probably I started skipping to not get called on, or to not, like, have to sit there looking dumb and everything, just having no idea what's going on. One class I remember skipping a lot was Spanish class. At first I was like, "Yeah, I get to learn Spanish." And then the first week went through and I was like, "I can't do this. This is horrible." And so I just, like, never went to that class.

There were times when I was away from school with friends where I did say, "Oh, yeah, I have to get back to school." 'Cause, like, school would call the house and everything if I was gone too long, and my mom would find out and stuff. If I skipped just, like, one class, my mom would be like, "Oh, why did you skip?" I would be like, "Oh, the teacher just forgot to put my attendance. I came in late."

My parents wanted me to go to school and everything, and I just wouldn't listen to them. I'd say, "Oh, yeah, I'm going to school." And I would get there, and I would see some people, and we would, like, hop in the car, go to someone else's house, or we would, like, go somewhere and eat breakfast or something like that. We would just leave and go hang out. And we would finally be like, "Oh, do you want to go back to school?" "Nah." "Me neither." I skipped probably, like, every day, like, a class a day.

I would say 9th grade I was in school probably three-fourths of the time. But 10th grade, I was there for half the time, maybe a little less than half. I left school probably a month or two before summer started. And I didn't drop out like a regular kid should, like, go in and get their notes. I just stopped going. So we started getting, like, mail from the court and all that. And then my mom was like, "Oh, well, you need to figure this out." So I finally went before school got over, and I un-enrolled myself.

If I think about it now, this year would have been my last year and I would be graduating by now. But I didn't think about it then, and I skipped all the time. When the counselor told me about an alternative school, I was just like, "But yeah, why do I need school? It's not teaching me what I need to know." So I stopped going to school.

Looking Back, Moving Forward

I was thinking of what I would do after I dropped out and everything. And for starters, I was like, "Maybe I should get my GED." I had told one of the teachers before about that and she said, "Oh, I have a GED book that helps you study for it." And so I looked at it, and it was just like, "Okay, if I definitely can't do school, then I definitely can't take this GED test." Because I looked at the book, and it was like a thick book and I thought, "I can't do this either."

And then I remember we had started talking about alternative school, like a college setting where people don't tell me what to do—maybe that would be a better placement for me. I wasn't really getting along with teachers. So I came and I found out that I started liking the alternative school. After a while, after I started getting to meet more people here, school just started being fun.

At this school, all the teachers are committed and help out and that's what I like. Like Mr. Hamilton, our math teacher, he always finds time for everyone in the class to help them out a little bit. And if you need the extra help, he'll, like, sit there and tell everyone to hold on while he helps the one person, like, catch up a little bit. And he'll make sure, he'll come back and check on you and stuff, and I really like that about him.

I was thinking about going and doing 2 years at college. But I'm not really sure of what I want to do yet or how my life is going. So, I'm just still trying to figure out what I want to do after high school, what's going to be, like, the thing I want to do.

CHAPTER 5

Teen Family and Personal Issues

In middle school I was more concentrated on trying to figure
out why my dad left. I feel like I was really a confused kid at that
point. . . . Also, the bullying started. —Trisha

For vulnerable students, teen years are a critical point of deflection onto a negative pathway toward dropping out of school. The previous two chapters focused on school-based factors that initiated and propelled students along this pathway. Most youth participants also struggled with serious challenges in their personal lives—challenges that significantly compounded their problems at school. In this chapter we look more closely at individual, family, and peer group issues that factored into pathways to dropping out. Some of these issues may have originated in childhood, but, as participants reported, they seemed to hit students hardest in adolescence.

Research on school risk factors recognizes that a range of personal issues (substance abuse, mental health problems, negative peer groups) and family issues (abuse, family dysfunction) are associated with a higher risk of school problems and dropping out (Rumberger & Lim, 2008). We sought to further explore the role these factors play in the dropping out process. The chapter begins with an overview of the kinds of personal challenges our study participants faced. We then look more closely at health, peer, and family issues—three areas that figured prominently in youths' stories about disengaging from and leaving school. These stories convey the powerful ways that personal vulnerabilities can become intertwined with and compound academic difficulties. Their stories might lead some to initially conclude that schools can do little to help these students. However, as we will explore further in Chapter 7, these stories provide clues to ways that schools can more effectively nurture and support struggling students despite their challenging personal circumstances.

OVERVIEW OF PARTICIPANT CHARACTERISTICS

Since our study focus was on the school-based experiences of youths who had dropped out, our interview protocol did not include questions about personal or family problems. Nonetheless, in the course of sharing their stories with us, interviewees spontaneously brought up personal experiences outside of school that they felt were germane to their dropping out process. Almost all the youths we interviewed revealed at least one significant personal challenge and could articulate how these personal challenges affected them in school.

As Figure 5.1 indicates, most resided in single-parent households, experienced behavioral problems at school, or engaged in significant alcohol or drug consumption before dropping out. In addition, over one third indicated they suffered from mental health issues, and one quarter had been removed from the home before reaching high school.

Figure 5.1. Participant Characteristics*

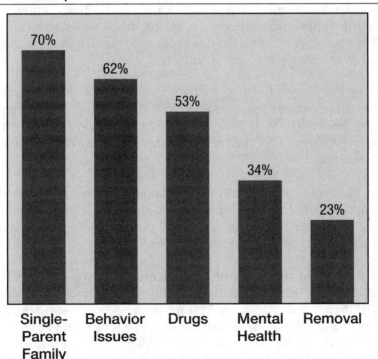

*(N = 53) Self-reported. Total exceeds 100% because students might appear in multiple categories.

HEALTH ISSUES

Many youth participants volunteered information about health issues connected to their flagging school participation. These issues ranged from problematic substance use and mental health struggles to physical health conditions (obesity, childhood diseases, injuries, pregnancy complications). This section considers how health-related problems appeared to trigger or worsen problems at school.

Alcohol and Drug Use

By far the most prevalent health-related issue reported was involvement with alcohol or drugs. Over half of participants told us they had engaged in early and/or regular consumption of alcohol or drugs, and described a pattern of drinking, smoking marijuana, or taking other drugs during the school day. They would consume illicit substances before school or leave school grounds to get high with friends and then not return. Alternatively, some actually would return to class, presumably unable to function well academically. At the time, many youths seemed to believe that drinking or taking drugs was simply a way to relax and have "fun"; they did not necessarily connect regular use with academic and family problems until later:

> I was 15, going to be 16, so in them ages you get introduced to drugs. You get introduced to partying. You get introduced to skipping school to go get high or to go have sex, or whatever the case may be. I'd say school wasn't as important to me anymore because I got sidetracked.
> —Yolanda

In hindsight, participants like Yolanda characterized their introduction to alcohol and/or drugs as a main factor leading to poor academic outcomes. However, their full narratives suggested a more complex set of circumstances. Echoing previous research findings (Breslau, 2010; Crosnoe, 2006), we discovered that school difficulties usually predated the onset of substance use. As we saw in Chapter 3, unaddressed learning challenges and other school problems typically initiated disengagement during the middle school years. Over time, this disaffection for school appeared to precipitate both truancy and substance abuse, more or less in tandem. In Jack's case, ongoing conflict at school, rather than academic issues, instigated a drinking problem:

> I felt like, "Okay, my home life is a bit hectic, but I can use school as
> my getaway." But once I got to high school and found that even there
> everything was so terrible, I had no getaway. And at that point I turned
> to drinking. And that just made everything fall to pieces right in front
> of me. —Jack

For a few youth participants, like Jack, substance use seemed to be a direct response to personal or family difficulties. More commonly, however, participants joined a peer group of similarly disengaged students, and the group encouraged illicit substance abuse. Later in this chapter we discuss the important role peers play in impelling vulnerable students toward truancy.

Mental Health Issues

In recounting their pathways to dropping out, about one third of interviewees mentioned mental health issues that became entangled with school problems. These issues included conduct disorders, anger management challenges, attention deficit disorder (ADD) or attention deficit hyperactivity disorder (ADHD), bipolar disorder, depression, and anxiety. They described bouts of anger, depression, anxiety, or other undiagnosed emotional conditions severe enough to cause them to feel unable to focus on school, complete homework, or even get out of bed. They missed classes and assignments, and failed tests and courses. Failure, in turn, increased anxiety and deepened depression, magnifying a sense of hopelessness about school. Youths often presented mental health problems as both a cause and an effect of school failure.

Mental health issues were frequently so bound up with school, family, or peer-related issues that the true etiology of the depression or anxiety remained uncertain. One pattern was clear: Reported mental health issues always co-occurred with significant drug or alcohol use, as was the case for Yolanda. At age 21, she was able to reflect on the deep connections between her placement in a group home as a preteen, the anger and depression that enveloped her over time, and her wish to escape from everything through "partying":

> I really didn't care anymore about anything. I was a child when I was
> taken away from my life, you know, the life that I was used to. I had
> a lot of hate and anger, a lot of depression. . . . I was a fucked-up kid,
> man. —Yolanda

Behavioral Issues

Behavioral issues at school appeared commonplace among participants, affecting roughly two thirds of the group. These issues resulted
in frequent disciplinary actions, school suspension, and expulsion. In
reflecting on the origins of their school problems, some participants believed that undiagnosed ADD/ADHD played a role. Others, like Derrick,
Xavier, and Jack, linked their problematic behavior directly to classroom and school contexts. Additionally, participants like Yolanda and
Jack endured extreme family dysfunction, which contributed to their
upsets at school. Regardless of the causes, behavioral issues often set up
a chain reaction of punishment, student resentment, further disengagement, and increased truancy.

From the youths' perspective, schools were less interested in understanding the backstories behind behavior and more interested in con-
trolling behavior through punishment. However, this approach rarely
addressed root causes driving the behavior, ensuring that the behavioral issue would be repeated. For example, Derrick confessed he was
constantly in trouble at school from 6th grade on, due to his classroom
antics, which in middle school were no longer tolerated:

> In my middle school, we had this thing called Positive Action. If you'd
> get in trouble in the middle of the class, you'd get a write-up, you
> know, and then they'd send you to a special room. I went to this room
> a lot. I was there probably every other day. I was being a class clown
> and just having fun, but the teachers wouldn't like it. —Derrick

Out-of-school suspension and expulsion were common responses
to many transgressions, including fighting, swearing, arguing with a
teacher, bringing drugs to school, and even (oddly enough) truancy. This "zero-tolerance" response was counterproductive because it
disrupted students' learning: Interviewees often reported being suspended for a week or more, during which time they typically were not
connected to academic supports. When they returned to school they
were substantially behind and unable to catch up, or they had missed
the end of a term and final exams. Moreover, these large blocks of out-
of-school time were generally unstructured, unsupervised time, providing more opportunities to hang out with others who were not in
school and further increasing the risk of delinquent behaviors (Hoeve
et al., 2009). In addition, suspensions negatively impacted motivation and behavior, especially when students interpreted suspension to
mean that they were not welcome at school. The role school discipline

policies appear to play in the dropping out process will be discussed further in Chapter 6.

Trauma and Loss

Themes of trauma and loss commonly appeared in participants' stories. Many had lost a parent through separation, divorce, abandonment, or death. Some had been neglected or abused, while others experienced serious family conflict, economic instability, or homelessness. In addition, a number were deeply affected by the loss of a close relative or friend. Although we did not probe into the details of what these experiences meant to the youths, they spontaneously described how personal losses devastated them emotionally, affecting their ability to focus on school:

> When I was in 8th grade, a close friend of mine died. I had known him since elementary school. I was a straight-A student until that point, and then I decided that I was just gonna check out. I decided that smoking pot and drinking was a way to help check out. —Callie

> My mother lost her life to the street, so I really was like, "Well fuck it, I'm not gonna be shit." My aunt evidently didn't give a fuck about me either: She put me in this group home bullshit. I was like, "Fuck life," you know? —Yolanda

As revealed in their full narratives, upon entering high school, Callie began skipping school regularly, and Yolanda quickly spiraled out of control.

Physical Health Conditions

We often do not associate physical health problems with dropping out, but research has uncovered a strong connection between health issues and school failure (Freudenberg & Ruglis, 2007). For almost a quarter of the young people we interviewed, physical health conditions, including pregnancy, miscarriage, illness, and injury, led to frequent or prolonged absences from school. Typically, these problems were not solely responsible for attendance and academic issues; these youths were already experiencing school difficulties prior to the onset of health issues. However, health problems created a new set of challenges for already struggling students. They missed classes, fell behind, became further discouraged, and failed classes they otherwise might have passed.

At the start of high school, Xavier, for example, faced medical issues that led to a cascade of new school problems:

> I messed up my shoulder. I had to miss school for, like, a week . . . and then, I had gotten mono right after . . . and that set me behind a lot. . . . I remember the principal calling me in and telling me . . . when I'm not here, they're not getting paid, so they have to withdraw me from school. . . . I felt like, man, I didn't wanna go to school. —Xavier

We do not know for certain what actually transpired with the school, but from Xavier's perspective, the school's unilateral move to withdraw him while he was recovering meant that he was unwelcome. After he re-enrolled, he began to act on his interpretation of events by skipping classes in earnest.

PEER INFLUENCES

Many participants reported joining peer groups that encouraged negative behaviors and magnified their existing vulnerabilities. Decades of delinquency research confirm the strong connection between socializing with delinquent peers and a host of undesirable outcomes during adolescence, including failing classes, dropping out of school, and becoming court-involved (Lipsey & Derzon, 1998). Youths' narratives help illustrate the mechanisms by which vulnerable students are drawn into negative peer groups and hence into truancy and other problem behaviors.

Social Skipping

Early truancy among youth participants typically was not a solitary activity but rather a social endeavor to be engaged in with other like-minded students or ex-students. Derrick explained how he routinely would check in with friends to make a date to skip school:

> My parents wanted me to go to school and everything, and I just wouldn't listen to them. I'd say, "Oh, yeah, I'm going to school." And I would get there, and I would see some people, and we would, like, hop in the car, go to someone else's house, or we would, like, go somewhere and eat breakfast. —Derrick

As described in Chapter 3, this early, more sporadic skipping behavior often went unchecked for a period of time. A lack of early and effective interventions created space for participants to form bonds with other disengaged peers, including those who had already dropped out. Joining in this "skipping culture" typically carried a host of negative consequences.

The Skipping Culture. As argued in previous chapters, in the majority of cases, a student's school problems tended to precede and precipitate truant behavior, not the reverse. Vulnerable students, including those who felt socially as well as academically excluded, were especially susceptible to the attractions of a skipping culture. Belonging to a peer group of fellow truants reinforced struggling students' rejection of school, thus encouraging further truancy. Offering a seemingly cool alternative to being in class, the group normalized skipping classes as something that was understandable and a viable, even irresistible alternative.

Later, youths who began having second thoughts about missing more and more school found it hard to exit the skipping culture. Group membership offered a lot to those who otherwise felt they did not belong: friendship, a social identity, and an immediate alternative to being unhappy in class or alone at lunch. Even if they came to feel that the group was leading them in the wrong direction, study participants did not necessarily see any alternatives. Who would they hang out with, if not with others who understood and shared their attitudes about school? Moreover, some admitted that if they tried to pull away, they felt intense counter-pressure from other group members to remain loyal.

Skipping and Substance Use. Being part of a skipping culture not only reinforced truancy but also seemed to encourage other problem behaviors, notably increasingly frequent alcohol and drug consumption. Youths were not always clear about the exact timing and causal relationships between substance use, early truancy, and participation in a skipping culture. However, their accounts suggest that many, including Derrick, Yolanda, Callie, and Xavier, were introduced to illicit substances directly through peers with whom they had started skipping:

> I think it was, like, probably the first semester, I started skipping a lot. I started smoking weed . . . started drinking. —Xavier

For some, like Yolanda, joining a skipping culture was a peer-sanctioned pathway to additional risky behaviors, including running away, having unprotected sex, and engaging in serious delinquency.

Serious Delinquency

A quarter of participants admitted to being gang-affiliated and/or involved in street crime, including theft, drug dealing, and prostitution
(the actual percentage could be higher because we did not ask directly
about peers outside of the school context). These individuals were more
likely to be accelerated leavers from school and to have:

- Experienced serious neglect, abuse, or other trauma
- Manifested significant behavioral issues at an early age
- Felt "pulled out" of school by the allure of the streets, rather
  than "pushed out"
- Delayed a return to an educational program for a long time
- Sought a GED rather than a diploma if and when they did
  finally return

Among the six young people we are following, Yolanda fit this profile exactly, having been consigned to various foster care situations from
an early age, struggling with depression, living on the streets, and engaging in prostitution and drug use:

> And that's when I started, like, running away from the group home,
> and then that's when I really wasn't attending school. I went to school,
> but I didn't go to school, so let's say I would go to school in the
> morning and, like, leave at, like, 11:00 A.M. I got in trouble a lot of the
> time, but I didn't care. —Yolanda

Yolanda is one of the more extreme cases of accelerated leavers we
encountered; it is easy to imagine why schools would find her a difficult
student to serve. However, in focusing on her very challenging personal
backstory, it is important to recall that her rocky transition to a new
school in 9th grade, described in Chapter 3, also played a role in her
pathway to dropping out.

FAMILY ISSUES

Significant family disruption or dysfunction plagued the majority of participants. In addition to painful losses of family members due to death,
divorce, incarceration, or abandonment, a sizable portion of the group
reported experiencing housing instability, parental neglect/abuse, foster

care challenges, or family conflict. Below are some of the main themes that cropped up in conjunction with family issues.

Ineffective Parental Responses to Problem Behavior

In hindsight, many youths wished they had listened more to their parents' pleas to stick with school. However, they portrayed parental responses to their early skipping and other problem behaviors as largely ineffective or nonexistent. Trisha, who struggled with academic failure, racial prejudice, and the absence of her biological father, felt her parents were trying their best to understand but "should have been more strict":

> I don't think my parents really knew what to do because I was their only child, and this was the first time that they were going through this. I think they kind of tiptoed and tried not to push me. I was never grounded or anything like that. —Trisha

The most common parental responses reported were verbal expressions of anger and disapproval. Some parents pleaded or tried to reason with the student, emphasizing the importance of attending school regularly. Sometimes parental reproaches or threats led to short-term improvements in attendance, especially if the school threatened to take the student and parent to truancy court. Despite these temporary improvements, interviewees inevitably reverted to skipping.

A number of youths portrayed their parents as unable to effectively monitor and control their behavior, thus providing the adolescents greater latitude to avoid homework, skip classes, and engage in other undesirable behaviors (Hoeve et al., 2009). According to interviewees, parents frequently seemed unaware of or unconcerned about the extent of the truancy, despite prior indications of a problem, such as letters or calls from the school, court truancy notifications, or failing grades. For example, after learning of his son's truant behavior, Jack's father (according to Jack) angrily berated him, and Jack temporarily stopped skipping school. However, since the underlying cause of his truancy (bullying) was not addressed, Jack soon resumed a pattern of regularly missing classes, yet claimed he suffered no further interference from either parents or the school for the remainder of the year.

As Jack's full narrative reveals, his chaotic, neglectful home situation was extreme, but even in families where parents displayed clear concern, participants claimed they were often able to circumvent efforts to monitor and control their behavior. Like many others, Derrick moderated his behavior after his parents received a truancy notice threatening court action. He skipped only one or two classes at a time afterward, and then if the school called, he made an excuse:

> If I skipped just, like, one class, my mom would be like, "Oh, why did you skip?" I would be like, "Oh, the teacher just forgot to put my attendance. I came in late." —Derrick

We cannot know for certain whether parents actually believed this kind of fabrication, but, in reflecting on their history of truancy, many youths thought this to be the case. From their stories, we infer that while many parents attempted to curb their children's skipping behavior, they did not seem to have the knowledge, personal background, or resources to be effective in sustaining these efforts. In some cases (at least 15% of interviewees' families), the parent was a refugee or immigrant facing cultural and/or linguistic barriers. In other cases, the parents' own experiences as a high school dropout may have influenced their ability to react to their children's school problems (Rumberger, 2011). Finally, some youths portrayed their early teen home life as dominated by housing instability, economic loss, or other family stressors. They did not necessarily connect these factors directly to a lack of effective parental guidance, discipline, or advocacy. However, we can surmise that these stressors consumed the time and attention of struggling parents, most of whom were single and therefore more likely to have limited personal and economic resources to call upon to help curtail their children's skipping behavior.

Parental Neglect, Abuse, and Abandonment

Over one third of interviewees reported experiencing serious family dysfunction, including neglect, abuse, parental mental illness, and addiction. They were more likely to be accelerated leavers who dropped out within a semester or year of starting to skip classes. Parental neglect at home overwhelmed and consumed even solid students like Jack, who at a young age had to assume a caretaker role in his family:

> My older sister had moved out by then, and my mom started drinking—I would get up early to wake my little brother up, make sure he got a shower and after he was done with the shower, I'd take my shower. Feed him breakfast, eat my breakfast, get us off to school. And then I'd have days where I'd come home, and then I'd have to take care of my mother. —Jack

A subset, like Yolanda, had spent time in foster care, historically one of the strongest predictors of negative educational and life outcomes (Day, 2011).

Family Instability and Conflict

Stepparents or new romantic partners brought additional stress into the household. Conflicts with a new authority figure in the home fueled emotional responses and behaviors that were counterproductive to school success, including fighting at school, running away, moving in with friends, or trying to live on one's own. Xavier, Yolanda, Jack, and Callie all reported experiencing family conflict that impacted them as young adolescents. Here is Callie's reflection on that time period:

> We'd moved in with my mom's boyfriend, then they'd get in fights; we'd have to move again. I was just so angry at her for that. I didn't like her boyfriend, and I was mad she kept going back to him. . . . It was just we were just butting heads and fighting over everything. . . . So I packed my stuff and left. —Callie

All too frequently, family-related stressors contributed to the youth's depression or anxiety; substance abuse typically ensued as well.

Virtually all of the youths were floundering in school by the time they entered 9th grade, yet, according to their accounts, few families appeared to have the personal or economic resources to address their children's needs. For example, not a single interviewee mentioned receiving individual academic tutoring (either through the school or through paid professional services) after they left elementary school. Only a handful of the many participants who described struggling with substance abuse or mental health issues indicated that they received professional services to help with these challenges. And few recalled their parents proactively trying to problem-solve with the schools on their behalf.

The absence of these kinds of supports tilted the playing field against students' school success (Rumberger, 2011). Participants' stories suggest many of them faced serious school challenges largely on their own, while at the same time contending with discouraging or even harmful relationships at home. But their stories would be incomplete without also mentioning some bright spots at school that buoyed them and, in some cases, helped them move toward graduation. These bright spots took the form of emotionally rewarding interactions with teachers and counselors, individuals who created safe and caring spaces for vulnerable students, the importance of which we discuss further in Chapter 7. Here is Jack describing a caring teacher he confided in:

> Mr. Brown was the only teacher I ever talked to about what was going on at home. And when I talked originally about dropping out, he actually pulled me aside after class. He sat me down and refused to let me leave the room until I promised him I'd finish my sophomore year.
> —Jack

After Jack dropped out, this same teacher helped him return to an alternative program to earn his diploma.

CONCLUSION

As we have argued throughout the book, no single factor appeared to trigger a serious pulling away from school. Rather, a perfect storm of family, individual, and school factors converged to overwhelm struggling students. This chapter illustrates the myriad nonacademic factors that commonly interfered with school success, including substance use, health problems, family dysfunction, and the negative influence of peers. Participants' narratives reveal several patterns regarding the interaction of school and nonschool factors. First, positive relationships with teachers in the early school years may have functioned as a protective factor for these vulnerable young people. Once their positive connections to adults dissipated in middle school, this key counterbalance to negative external forces was lost.

Second, narrative patterns belie the notion that adolescents "bring" their individual problems, such as substance abuse and delinquent behavior, to school, thus initiating academic or other school problems. For most students, the opposite seemed to be the case: Significant issues at school precipitated their early stages of disengagement, followed by induction into a skipping culture and near simultaneous initiation into the world of drugs, alcohol, and, in some cases, serious delinquency.

Third, academic and nonacademic problems often became tightly intertwined. Schools alone might not be able to do much about certain external influences on students. However, as we argue in the final chapter, the ways in which schools respond to students' challenges ultimately matter a great deal to those students' outcomes.

Jack's Story

Jack is Caucasian and from a rural high school with a high dropout rate. He is a wiry, intense young man sporting a ragged untrimmed beard and torn shirt. Jack is a voracious reader, loves intellectual argument, and is passionate about music. By the time Jack reached middle school, there were no longer any stable caretakers at home. From the age of 14 onward he essentially raised himself and his younger brother on his own. He worried constantly about his ability to carry out the adult responsibilities that had been thrust upon him. By 10th grade his academic performance had begun to slip, and what had been sporadic bullying intensified; these factors, in addition to challenges at home, pushed Jack toward dropping out of school.

Early School Years

When I was in 1st grade probably up until 5th grade I'd say I really looked forward to going to school. Because, to me, it was just a time to hang out with my friends and, you know, do whatever little classwork there was, then go out to lunch, recess. Fifth grade was before, you know, being too nerdy made you unpopular. And it was also before everybody was worried about, you know, what everybody looked like or how you dressed—because we were kids enjoying having time with our friends. And to me that was a treasurable time in my life.

I actually learned how to read before I entered kindergarten. I read *The Matrix* in the 3rd grade. And it took me months because there were words in there, I didn't know what they were. I had to go by what the context was, to try to figure out the definition. I'd just read the sentence over and over again and think, "Okay, that word means something—what does it mean in this context?" And just based on what they're writing about—what the characters are saying—this helped me to figure out what the word meant.

My favorite classroom activity, besides reading, was writing. We'd start off every day in 3rd grade with writing. We'd just write about how our day is going or do a free write on something. And just to be able to sit there and write everything out and not feel like I was gonna get in trouble for something I wrote about—that's what I liked. I still am very much into writing.

When I was younger I wanted to be the best at everything because I thought that's how I was supposed to be. It was actually kind of frustrating because I wanted—at that point in time—I wanted to learn more. I was just a sponge ready to soak up all this information, and it felt like I was up front and everyone else was behind me, and I felt like I had to wait for them to catch up instead of someone helping them out more to catch up to me. So as far as, you know, being born smart and then working hard to learn, I think it's really a mixture of both. You're born with the ability to attain so much knowledge, and then you surpass that level by working harder to gain more knowledge.

Mrs. Miller was my favorite teacher. Because she knew how I was such a bookworm. In the classroom she kept her own personal collection. And she would let me take a book home over the weekend. I'd finish the entire book, bring it back, and get another one. And I did that for my entire 1st-grade year. She was very loving, very caring, very nurturing with everybody and really, you know, encouraged creativity in everybody. And she was by far one of my biggest influences on my creativity. She taught me about music.

Middle School Challenges

Seventh grade was my first year with my band teacher, Mr. Sanchez. He really kind of pointed me in the right direction with music and taught me so much stuff. I really respect him. And our band was really good. He seemed like one of the only teachers at that school that really cared about me. Yeah, we just developed a really close relationship.

I was still a good student in middle school. The only class I struggled with was science. For some reason, I could never wrap my mind around the concepts of science. Eighth grade was when I first was introduced to the periodic table of elements; everything went right over the top of my head, and I would work and work to try and understand it, but I just never could.

At the time all the classes in middle school were overfull. They didn't have enough teachers for all the students. So in my science class there were 34 students for one teacher. And that situation was just out of hand. You could never get one-on-one time with the teacher. Because when you go to raise your hand and ask a question, you're followed by 11 other people. My science teacher was pretty good. There were just not enough hours in the day for him to be able to get to everybody who needed help.

My 8th-grade year was actually simple because at that point I knew I was going to get picked on at school because I was a nerd. Kids always try to pick fights with other people. I don't know if it was to show dominance or something. I don't know, but they always started stuff with somebody. There was always drama with somebody. So I avoided everyone, and I just stuck to my classwork. And then after school I went straight home, took care of everything there, came back, and did the same thing all over again. But I almost became robotic. My life was just all a schedule. I just did what I had to do and moved on.

Navigating High School

I went from junior high to actual high school in 10th grade. My chances to read were very few and far between, but sophomore year was good in some ways. I had a teacher by the name of Mr. Brown, who was by far the best teacher I had at that high school. And he introduced me to a lot of Shakespearean stuff. I absolutely fell in love with the writing and just the way it was all, you know, phrased. And the subtle, inappropriate things that are in a play just made me chuckle. And that really brought back my love for writing—because that's when I started writing, reading a lot more, writing more poetry and song lyrics and stuff.

Being able to do the work wasn't an issue as long as I was in the classroom. But once I got to like homework and things I had to bring home to do, at that point everything was so crazy there was never any time for it. I'd be rushing last minute—riding the school bus trying to get everything done, and it never worked out. I couldn't work at home, so really the only work I got done was while I was in class.

My older sister had moved out by then, and my mom started drinking. My dad wasn't around much by then. So while she was a mess—I was the oldest person in the house—the oldest kid in the house and I had to—I would get up early to wake my little brother up, make sure he got a shower and after he was done with the shower, I'd take my shower. Feed him breakfast, eat my breakfast, get us off to school. And then I'd have days where I'd come home and then I'd have to take care of my mother, wait for my little brother to get home from school, take care of him—and it pretty much became me raising my mother.

Mr. Brown was the only teacher I ever talked to about what was going on at home. And when I talked originally about dropping out, he actually pulled me aside after class. He sat me down and refused to let me leave the room until I promised him I'd finish my sophomore year.

I felt like, "Okay, my home life is a bit hectic, but I can use school as my getaway." But once I got to high school and found that even there everything was so terrible, I had no getaway. And at that point I turned to drinking. And that just made everything fall to pieces right in front of me.

I didn't start to skip classes until after winter break. That was the point at which everything was just unbearable, and I started skipping on a regular basis. I would ditch school with my skateboard and go to the mall. At school I couldn't find any release, couldn't find any release at home.

At the time skateboarding with my headphones on—that was the most freedom I ever felt. Because I didn't have to kick and push, or anything, just cruise around. So at that point, skipping was my release.

At one point I skipped almost 2 weeks straight and they'd called my dad. He chewed me out and said they were going to possibly take me to truancy court. So for about a month I went to school every day and then I would skip 1 day out of the week and the next time I'd skip 2 days out of the week—next week, you know—1 day out of the week. I just kept alternating like that. But at the time school was not any more pleasant for me than home was.

They never brought truancy court up again. I missed up to 40% of my classes that second semester. I'm sure the school called home again, but I don't know if they ever reached anybody. My dad was gone by then, and my mother was drinking so heavily at the time I'd be surprised if she could hear the sound of her own voice.

Early high school I was on the nerdy side. I was a bookworm, and I got picked on a lot. That's what caused me to leave high school. Like, I'd be walking to go to my locker and someone would just put their foot out and trip me. I always thought that only happened in the movies. And it was like everybody tried to fight everybody. When I was in high school, there was a fight every day between somebody, and I got tired of it.

People picking on me continued until I'd say three-quarters of the way through 10th grade, which was when everything that had built up exploded. The wrong group of people decided to mess with me on the wrong day, and I just snapped. I completely lost it. And I'm very much a pacifist. I don't believe that fighting is necessary in any situation. And the fact that I put hands on another individual shocked me more than it shocked anybody else.

The school was totally aware of what had been happening. I'd been going and telling the principal, telling my counselor—all these people—telling so many people that I was constantly being picked on. The principal and vice principal, they're very nonactive players in the school, I'd have to say. They prefer to just sit in their office and leave it to everybody else to handle. Nobody did anything. I didn't see what else I could do. I got suspended for 2 weeks because I stood up for myself after three-quarters of a year of being picked on. Since I threw the first punch, the school just said I had assaulted the others. They threatened to throw me in juvie, but then suspended me instead.

It was, like, the last month of school and I had been skipping a lot. I came back on the last day of school only to have someone try to pick on me. And I snapped once again and at that point I just knew I couldn't go back to that school.

I didn't get into trouble because school had officially ended and I was at the mall right afterwards and then those kids came over and that whole altercation started. So they couldn't—the school was technically out, it wasn't the school year, so I couldn't get in trouble there. But I knew I couldn't be at that school for 2 more years. So I just never went back.

My teacher, Mr. Brown, had told me about online school before I left. And he said, "I know you have troubles in a regular school environment, but this is a school, fully accredited and you can get your high school diploma here." This stuck with me because at that time he was the only one whose word I could trust.

I managed to get enrolled at the online school a while later. There you met once a week with the teacher and class through videoconferencing, so instead of having to sit through a full day of classes, the rest of the time you did it on your own. It was self-study at your own pace, and they offered a lot more extensive classes than the regular high school did. I just motored through everything so I could get all the credits I needed for my full junior year in just 1 semester. I completed my senior year, as well, and got my diploma that way.

Looking Back, Moving Forward

Originally I had no intention of ever going back to school. But now that I have my diploma I want to go to college. I'm currently applying to schools. I was going to go to community college here near town, but the classes they offer are so limited, and I didn't feel it was enough for me to be able to dedicate myself to going there. I haven't decided whether I want to do literature or psychology as my major. But either way, I want to study both.

I wish someone could have listened to me and done something about what was happening to me. My grandmother tried once to help. She caught me skipping one day and she took me back to her house, and we sat down and talked about everything for a few hours. She offered me a place to live with her, but she didn't have room for both me and my little brother. And she wanted to call and have us both put in foster care, and I wouldn't let her do that. At that point I pretty much just stopped trying to go to people for help.

Someone could have done something about my getting picked on at school, instead of just saying, "Well, it happens, it's high school." That was always their excuse. "This is how high school is, it's not easy for everybody. It's high school, deal with it." And to me that wasn't good enough. I had people I was friends with who tried to kill themselves because of stuff that happened in high school—all the bullying. And to me seeing all this happen and the fact that even after—I mean attempted suicide, that's about the biggest cry for help there is in this world. And even after that they don't do anything about it? They don't step up and try to make a change? It's horrible, it's sad, and it seems to be the way of the world anymore. And it's a world I don't understand.

Callie's Story

Callie, who is Caucasian, was raised in a small town. An energetic and expressive young woman, she was eager to participate in the study, hoping her story would help teachers better understand what vulnerable youth need in order to succeed in school. She loved her early elementary years, particularly reading and writing activities. School went well for her until the end of middle school, when the death of a close friend catapulted her into turmoil and trouble—she began skipping school and drinking. In addition, Callie contended with pregnancy and a turbulent home life. During high school she transferred multiple times, searching for an educational setting that would allow her to regain her footing and to progress toward graduation, but obstacles kept getting in her way.

Early School Years

Until the 8th grade, I loved school. I loved learning. I loved everything about school. I didn't care what we were learning. For me it was, "We're learning something and I'm gonna do great." And school was just incredible to me. It was like magic back then. I always excelled. I had an older sister, so she was already going to school. So we'd go to school together. I remember, you know, her trying to help me because she was three grades ahead of me. And so, it wasn't just that I was learning. It's that my sister was helping me, and I was learning faster because I had an older kid on my side. School was just incredible to me. It was like magic back then.

In kindergarten, they wanted me to go up a grade because I wouldn't do my work in the books because I already knew everything, but my mom wanted me to stay in my same age group. She used to read to us every night. It was, you know, always one of my favorite things. Probably that is why I wanted to learn how to read because I thought it was just so incredible. I don't remember what we were required to read in school, but I remember checking out as many books as I could from the library. I loved to read. I always have. I can express myself and transport myself to a new world in a book. And that was life changing.

My 1st-grade teacher was my favorite teacher. I know we used to use, like—we'd have these cool erasers on our pencils, and we'd point to the letters and the words like that. Later in elementary school I was learning more and faster, and I was getting more excited about middle school and high school and what I could do in the future. All of these possibilities started running through my head. I started learning better math and better writing and better reading and started learning about science, and I was just so excited to learn in elementary school!

We did science projects. We did this thing with water and oil and food coloring and put it in a bottle. And then, we hooked another bottle to it and screwed them together. And we added, like, sand and stuff and it taught us about the density of different liquids, and it was just—I was always better with hands-on learning. So that was—I was actually learning something. I had friends during elementary school, too. I wasn't in the popular crowd, but I was just, like, in the middle. I had my group of friends, and we all looked out for each other, and we were all good.

Middle School Challenges

Well, middle school was a little bit harder. I thought I was prepared for it, because in 6th grade we had started switching classes. We'd have math and science with one teacher and the other classes with another one. And I was like, "Yeah, this is gonna be easy!" But then, in 7th grade, instead of having only one teacher give you all the homework, it was each teacher giving you a little bit of homework. And then, you had to deal with all these different classes with all these different teachers. A lot more moving around, a lot more different classes. There were more course options, and it was just . . . overwhelming.

I was trying my hardest, and I would get upset if I didn't get a good grade. And I was straight A's all through 7th and part of 8th grade. Reading is something that I've always excelled in. I got pretty shy with presentations and stuff because I get shy with oral presentations. But I did pretty good.

Math has never been a strong suit for me. So going from simple multiplication and division, which I already knew but was still pretty hard for me—going from that to learning algebra was like I was thrown into a whole other dimension of math. I had to do a study group. I had to get all this extra help from my mom and from my sister, and I was still not getting it. That was one of the biggest problems for me because I was getting B's and C's on the algebra tests and stuff. I was getting really upset because I couldn't try any harder. If the class had gone a little bit slower, I probably would have done a lot better.

The teacher just didn't understand how everybody's not on the same level. I was listening and everything, but I just wanted her to say the explanation again or something, but the teacher just wouldn't. She's telling me instead to ask somebody next to me. That person is not telling me.

If algebra class had been slowed down—if it wasn't just, okay, 8 squared plus B squared equals X, it wasn't—I mean, that wasn't middle school math. But if it wasn't just, like, thrown on you. It was so confusing. I was trying to get help from my older sister, but she hadn't learned the math yet because they had changed curriculums. So it was like I was learning something in 7th grade that my 10th-grade sister still hadn't learned yet. And I was just like, "You've got to be kidding. I need help!"

I was also bored because the teachers make you sit there and listen while they read. And they have a monotone voice, and it's just, like, putting me to sleep. And I hated the textbooks. Why not, like, go outside more if you're in science, learning about plants? Go look at the real plants instead of looking at them in books.

When I was in 8th grade, a close friend of mine died. I had known him since elementary school. I was a straight-A student until that point, and then I decided that I was just gonna check out. I decided that smoking pot and drinking was a way to help check out. So I focused more on doing things that were very bad for me instead of focusing on trying to improve my life. I just stopped caring. Well, a lot—a lot of people had the same reaction. We were all just kind of in a funk. And so, a lot of us weren't doing nearly as well as we had in the first place. Even the teachers, they kind of backed off a little. We still had to finish the curriculum, but it seemed like they'd kinda slowed down for us.

Navigating High School

By the time I got to high school I would go to class if I thought it was fun. I would only go to school on the days where I had photography. I liked that class and I got to express myself. But the other classes, it was, "I don't care." Whatever we're learning in math, they teach it once and then you just have to, like, do it by yourself or figure it out, how to do it on your own, right? So, I didn't like that. I think it was the homework part too, the homework and then having to bring it back in. By the time I got home and I was ready to do my homework, that class period was already fading away, and I was forgetting how to do things. I was in that area where I—if it was fun, sure, I'll go to class. But other than that, I wanted to hang out. "I wanna smoke pot and I wanna drink." I just kept doing that until I went to court for truancy.

I didn't wanna drop out. I had a lot of extenuating circumstances that made it difficult for me to graduate, and eventually, it was just too much. I had to stop, but my biggest goal all throughout life was to graduate high school. I was really disappointed that I didn't graduate.

There wasn't somebody who had my back going, "You're doing good." I didn't have that extra push, and that's something that I've always needed is that, "You need to do this." But there was nobody really that I could turn to because they didn't have the time or they weren't really all there. And then, it kinda made me realize, "Oh, I'm really not going anywhere with my life right now. I really need to stop and look back on what's going on."

When I was skipping, my mom was gonna send me away to live with my aunt and uncle unless I got into Benson [alternative high school]. I applied, but they didn't let me in. My grades were not bad enough for me to need the extra help, which doesn't make sense. My best friend was going to Benson at the time. She knew if I didn't get to go to Benson, I would just drop out. So she talked to her teachers. And the teachers talked to the principal, and then they let me in.

I finally got interested in school. I had a part in the decisionmaking, and we actually got a say in certain aspects of what we would do. I wanted to go and I was excited about homework, which hadn't happened since 6th grade. The teachers, they understood we were teenagers.

I've also never been a fan of government or politics. I remember I didn't like it, and I complained about that class for the first 3 weeks. And my teacher, he finally—he comes out with this project. We write—we pretend that we are a person in that time. And we have to do a journal with a map kind of like Christopher Columbus, except I don't think that's who it was. But I got all excited, and so I went and got, like, a leather notebook thing. I made sure I used, like, a fancy pen, and I tried to write in cursive and I got to use my creative writing skills. But I also had to do the research for it.

I was working really hard at Benson. After skipping a lot, I started taking extra classes and working twice as hard. And then, at 17 I got pregnant. It got confirmed, but then I was in the hospital because I miscarried. Then after that, I moved out of my mom's house. She and I hadn't gotten along since before when I decided that I was checking out. We'd moved in with my mom's boyfriend, then they'd get in fights; we'd have to move again. I was just so angry at her for that. I didn't like her boyfriend, and I was mad she kept going back to him.

And because my mom also had problems at the time, she took this already bad situation and she just exploded. So we never really talked

about things and came to common ground. It was just we were just
butting heads and fighting over everything.

It was just constant chaos. So I packed my stuff and left. And then
I was working and paying rent and going to school. That became hard
because I had a full-time job that was night shift, so school kinda went
on the back burner . . . and then, I was—I lost that job. So I decided that,
okay, I'm gonna get back in gear.

Then, it was like I moved again, and I moved in with my friend Bonnie.
It was just, like, constant—everything just kept changing for me. One
thing after another kept happening. It was like I really wanted to graduate
but there was so much that was going on that made it so difficult to
focus on school when I—I mean, it was hard to get out of bed in the
morning. It's like, even though I worked really, really hard and did, like,
double classes for 2 years straight, I was just like, "I can't deal with this."

Another big thing about not being able to finish was they got rid of
Benson. That more personal experience, being able to be closer with the
teachers and have more one-on-one was what I needed for high school.
I developed a relationship with all three of the teachers I had. Even now
when I have problems, I still come and talk to them because I've known
them for 6 years. And the school really was a family, and it's like that's
what I needed.

So them getting rid of that school that I came to know as this—this
Benson family—they got rid of that. And it was just like I was floating
almost. I actually did try online school for a few months, but I couldn't
do it because there wasn't one-on-one help. There wasn't—it was—"It's
me and a computer and I need to push myself and I don't." If I had a
question, it could take a day before I would get an answer to it. I had to
figure it out for myself, and nobody showed me how to use the classes
that were online. I was really confused. I couldn't even figure out how to
turn an assignment in. It didn't work. So I stopped trying.

Looking Back, Moving Forward

Right now I'm focusing mainly on my GED so I can have that done and
out of the way. What I want to do more than anything is help people.
That's what I've always wanted to do, and right now I'm thinking
of becoming a teacher because I would love to make a difference in
somebody's life, like my teachers made in mine. I'm just kind of weighing
my options right now. Then, once I get that I'm gonna start looking into
general classes that you need for multiple different degrees and start
slowly taking those.

I moved back to my mom's house, actually, a few months ago. She
pulled herself together, and I stopped doing inappropriate things, and I

started to open up to her. I don't keep secrets from her anymore. I have some medical bills I need to pay off, and I need to get my GED and all that taken care of before I start trying to get a loan to go to college. I wanna just get everything straightened out before I start making a mess again.

I love the idea of having you talk to people that have dropped out because everyone's got their different stories . . . I think that doing this is gonna help somebody else to graduate. So I really love this idea.

CHAPTER 6

Exiting School

> It was like I really wanted to graduate but there was so much that was going on that made it so difficult to focus on school when I—I mean, it was hard to get out of bed in the morning. It's like, even though I worked really, really hard and did, like, double classes for 2 years straight, I was just like, "I can't deal with this." —Callie

By the time youth participants were in high school, truancy and course failure had become the norm. Whether they recognized it or not (and some seemed not to), they were now clearly at risk for leaving school. This chapter follows our participants in the final phase of dropping out. The first section of the chapter explores "tipping points," crucial events and circumstances that impacted the decision to stop attending school. Many of these tipping points, like insufficient credits to graduate or an unintended pregnancy, are well documented in the research literature; however, other factors emerged as well. Participants' stories at this last stage reveal much about how youths interpreted their circumstances, why they finally chose to leave, and the complexities of this process.

The second part of the chapter focuses on participants' educational experiences after they dropped out. Some returned to a new educational setting only to drop out again fairly quickly, while others were more successful in finding a pathway toward graduation. We explore factors that might explain these different educational trajectories and conclude the chapter with participants' reflections about dropping out.

TIPPING POINTS

In reflecting on their pathways to dropping out, students identified what they believed to be clear *tipping points* that terminated their connection to school, adding one final event to the complex web of factors that had pushed them down the pathway to dropping out of school. Tipping points youths identified include:

- Serious academic failure
- Expulsion and suspension
- Bullying
- Housing instability or homelessness
- Health issues
- Pregnancy
- Gang membership or delinquent activity

Although participants often identified a single tipping point associated with dropping out, that point typically represented the culmination of multiple unaddressed academic, behavioral, peer, and personal issues. In the following sections, we discuss each tipping point separately, while acknowledging that a complex process involving myriad factors often led to any given tipping point.

Serious Academic Failure

One of the most frequent explanations for dropping out was that students had already failed too many classes and, at some point, became hopeless about their situation. Participants often conveyed a sense of being trapped in a "Groundhog Day"[1] scenario in which failure in one form or another was repeated over and over again at school. Especially as they grew older and fell further behind in credits, many youths gave up rather than trying to continue. As Trisha posed rhetorically after recounting her multiple failures, "What was the point [of continuing in school]?" These findings echo those of other studies that consistently have found that academic failure is a top reason students give for quitting school (Rotermund, 2007).

Students who left after successive academic failures were not cavalier about these failures; most took them very much to heart, feeling inadequate and "stupid." They frequently blamed themselves for not trying harder and made a clear connection between missing so much school, failing, and giving up. When we asked students about their decisions, they often would provide explanations similar to Yolanda's:

I don't know what I was thinking about my future or what my life would be like. No one I know that didn't graduate has ever tried to tell other kids they don't need to. In fact, all of us really regret it. —Yolanda

Slow faders constituted much of the group that said they left primarily because of academic failure. Accelerated leavers like Yolanda also experienced multiple course failures prior to dropping out. However, they perceived other factors to be more significant in shaping their decision to leave school. Remarkably, a number of slow faders reflected that even after failing multiple core courses needed for graduation, they still pictured themselves finishing high school on time, seemingly oblivious to their precarious position and lack of academic progress. They maintained hope that somehow they would graduate while, at the same time, continuing to skip and fail classes.

Xavier followed this contradictory pattern of remaining fully committed to the *idea* of graduating, but not fully committed to school. After a mini-dropout at the start of his senior year, Xavier improved attendance and grades, but still lacked the credits needed to graduate. At almost 19 years old, he decided to return for a 5th year of high school but found he could not sustain his motivation:

> I hated the environment at the school. It was just really strict. And it was just that I was older; I didn't like being treated like a kid. —Xavier

Fortunately, Xavier was not out of school for long. He was able to transfer to an alternative educational setting that offered individual support, opportunities for credit retrieval, and a more relaxed learning environment that better suited his needs.

Expulsion and Suspension

Research suggests a correlation between exclusionary school discipline policies, such as expulsion or out-of-school suspension, and increased dropout rates (Fabelo et al., 2011; Skiba & Peterson, 1999). Our interview data support this basic connection: About a quarter of youth interviewees linked a specific discipline event to dropping out. They described two ways in which school discipline policies and events impacted their ability and/or desire to stay in school.

First, serious discipline events almost always resulted in severe academic consequences. In line with the findings of others (Fabelo et al., 2011), interviewees who had been suspended or expelled reported that their schools rarely provided alternative educational settings for them during their exclusion. Suspensions in high school often lasted 2 weeks or longer, virtually guaranteeing that students would lose credit for at least some of their classes and have to repeat them. Structurally, short-term suspension proved to be similarly detrimental academically: Youths described having to report to a monitored room where they were expected to do assignments on their own, isolated from any substantive instructional support. For students who were already disengaged from school and doing poorly academically, suspension or expulsion sometimes became the final tipping point: After being required to leave, students simply opted not to return to school.

Second, punished students frequently believed that they had been unfairly treated by the school, that decisionmakers did not take into account the sources or causes of their behavior, or that school officials simply did not listen or care. Jack, Trisha, and Xavier all recounted incidents when they had been bullied or goaded by other students into lashing out, but they ended up receiving equal or harsher punishment than those provoking them. Such experiences reduced their trust in school as a fair institution looking out for the interests of all students.

Bullying

In Chapter 4 we portrayed how widespread and damaging school bullying was to participants, inflicting emotional pain, interfering with learning, and inducing victims to skip school. Not surprisingly, then, ongoing bullying often led to a tipping point. In some cases the connection between bullying and dropping out was more indirect: Victims might become academically disengaged, miss important assignments, and lose such a large number of credits that they gave up. For others, like Jack, the connection was direct: After being suspended for lashing out at the students who had been tormenting him, he barely attended. From his perspective, school personnel could have addressed the relentless bullying—but didn't.

> Someone could have done something about my getting picked on at school, instead of just saying, "Well, it happens, it's high school." That was always their excuse. . . . And to me that wasn't good enough. I had people I was friends with who tried to kill themselves because of stuff that happened in high school—all the bullying. —Jack

Housing Instability and Homelessness

More than a third of youth interviewees revealed they had experienced unstable living situations. Some endured high levels of economic distress and/or family disruption, resulting in multiple moves and school transfers that indirectly or directly instigated dropping out. Others simply stopped going to school after yet another move to a new school or district.

Family strife sometimes caused youths to live on their own, with no parental guidance or support. In some cases, a parent's new partner led to either the youth or the parent moving out. In other cases, participants became homeless because they ran away or were kicked out. This kind of household instability often coincided with academic failure and dropping out; their dire living circumstances made it nearly impossible for students to continue with school, even if they were motivated to do so.

Yolanda experienced a rapid and permanent break from school by running away from her group home at the end of 9th grade and living on the streets as an underage prostitute for 8 months. She reflected that she ran away in order to escape a confining, uncaring situation and to experience "freedom" from adult authority and school demands:

> Like, I don't understand why I was at the group home for so long because I was like, "I'm at the age where you guys really can't tell me shit no more." I'm running away. I'm not going to school. I'm doing drugs. I'm having sex. —Yolanda

Health Issues

As described in Chapter 5, substance abuse, health, and mental health issues cropped up frequently in participants' depictions of their early stages of disengagement from school. In some instances these problems worsened over time, causing serious disruptions at home and at school. Interestingly, national surveys that asked students about their reasons for leaving school did not report either substance abuse or mental health as primary reasons given (Rotermund, 2007). In contrast, some of the young people we interviewed considered a drug or mental health issue as the major cause for leaving school. They described being too continually under the influence to attend class and complete assignments or too depressed to get out of bed day after day. At a certain point, the motivation to stay in school vanished. Trisha, who struggled academically, suffered racial prejudice and bullying, and endured a family breakup, ultimately ascribed dropping out to her depressed emotional state:

> I just ended it with the alternative school after I turned 18—just not really going anymore. What was the point? I would stay at home and sleep all day. —Trisha

Pregnancy

A handful of young women we interviewed described being pregnant during high school and consistently identified pregnancy as the tipping point leading to their departure from school. This finding aligns with national student surveys showing that physical health complications, like morning sickness, make daily attendance at school difficult (Rotermund, 2007). Other disengagement factors, such as academic failure, were already in play for these young women before they became pregnant, so pregnancy may have expedited the way out from an already aversive situation. Most, however, conveyed that they dropped out due to the *social stigma* attached to their condition; they felt negatively judged by peers or school staff, or feared they would be, creating an added pressure to quit school.

Callie was one of the young women who became pregnant and dropped out, but her story differed from others in certain respects. Her pregnancy not only resulted in serious complications, but also was coupled with additional personal setbacks that overwhelmed her at a critical moment when she was trying to get back on track at school:

> I was in the hospital because I miscarried. Then after that, I moved out of my mom's house. . . . And then I was working and paying rent and going to school. That became hard because I had a full-time job that was night shift, so school kinda went on the back burner. —Callie

Callie's story illustrates how the convergence of disparate personal challenges creates terrible pressures that lead struggling students to a tipping point. Although she subsequently attempted to return to school a couple of times after these setbacks, she was unable to accomplish her goal of graduating.

Gangs or Criminal Activity

Yolanda faced many serious personal challenges (neglect, abandonment, mental illness, self-destructive behaviors), but her general profile and dropping out pattern was not unique. A quarter of all participants (most of whom also had experienced unstable, neglectful, or abusive home situations) gravitated to gangs or individuals that engaged in illegal activities. Through these affiliations, they were drawn into street crimes, including prostitution, drug dealing, theft, and gang activity. They did not always directly link their participation in criminal activity to leaving school, but the two conditions often occurred within a short period of time.

In addition to lacking support and stability at home, this subset of youth participants appeared to have a history of academic and attendance problems, early delinquency, and persistent behavior issues. In reflecting on the decision to leave school, they portrayed themselves not so much as *pushed out* by the school as *pulled out* by peers. Like Yolanda, they made it clear that the allure of street life was much more powerful than any attraction school (or home) might have to offer; a life on the streets felt more "free," adult, and powerful. They were mostly accelerated leavers, dropping out quickly at a young age. Unlike many slow faders, these youths did not, at the time, subscribe to general societal values about the importance of school. However, like most other participants, they later deeply regretted the decision they had made to leave school.

DROPPING OUT PATTERNS

Although tipping points often capture the moment in which young people take the final step in dropping out of school, underlying patterns of dropping out start with an initial disengagement from school and may include myriad factors in a complex process spanning many years. Youths' stories suggest the end of this process is also complex and not as clear-cut as one might suppose it to be.

Truant or Dropped Out?

We have focused largely on dropping out as a unidirectional process encompassing four phases and culminating in a final exit. However, for many interviewees, the process was less well-defined. To begin with, participants themselves were not always sure of their status. Some, like Derrick, left school without giving any formal notification; he considered himself to be out of school, whereas the school considered him to be truant:

> I left school probably a month or two before summer started. And I didn't drop out like a regular kid should, like, go in and get their notes. I just stopped going. So we started getting, like, mail from the court and all that. —Derrick

Others, like Xavier (whose unintentional disenrollment is referred to in Chapter 5), never intended to "drop out," but for various reasons (e.g., extended absences, detention or incarceration, expulsion) school unilaterally withdrew them. Technically, they might be considered dropouts, but they did not always view themselves as such.

Dropping In, Dropping Out

Dropping out was frequently a temporary act: Over time, many participants moved back and forth on a truancy–dropout continuum, attending for a period and then not attending. In Chapter 1, we introduced the pattern of "serial dropping out," that is, dropping out, re-enrolling, then dropping out again. At least half of participants told us that after dropping out they re-enrolled, usually in a different school, but still aiming for a diploma. Among our profiled youths, all but Trisha followed this pattern of attempting a return to high school. For reasons we will touch upon below, participants who re-enrolled often fared no better in the new setting, whether it was a traditional or an alternative school. They returned to truant behavior and then dropped out again. We interviewed young people who had repeated this cycle three and even four times.

Callie, for example, re-enrolled three separate times in three different educational settings, owing to her extreme truancy in 9th grade and other periods of complete nonattendance during high school. She had been happy and productive for a time when she transferred to an alternative school setting, but as described in her full narrative, after a series of personal tragedies, she dropped out and never quite regained her momentum. Her last attempt was with an online option available in her district:

> I actually did try online school for a few months, but I couldn't do it because there wasn't one-on-one help. . . . I was really confused. I couldn't even figure out how to turn an assignment in. It didn't work. So I stopped trying. —Callie

Like many others who followed this repetitive dropping in, dropping out pattern, she ultimately gave up on seeking a diploma and instead was pinning her hopes on obtaining a GED certificate at some point.

SUCCESSFUL AND UNSUCCESSFUL RE-ENROLLMENT IN SCHOOL

Why, after dropping out, did some participants manage to find a pathway back toward graduation, while others did not? Their narratives provide clues as to what motivated them to stick with school the second (and sometimes third) time they enrolled. Conversely, other narratives suggest why many were unable to persevere in new school settings.

Unsuccessful Returns

Participants' discussions of their unsuccessful attempts to return to school revolved around two major themes. First, those who were unsuccessful (including those who did not even try to return) often faced serious personal problems, such as addiction, emotional difficulties, or family conflict. As described in Chapter 5, such issues significantly influenced their dropping out process and remained largely unaddressed. When vulnerable youths entered a new educational program but still lacked the personal supports required to succeed, they floundered once again. Yolanda described her post–dropping out return to an alternative program:

> After being on the street for a while, I tried a school program. That didn't work out, though, because too much of a bad crowd went to that program. So as you can most likely guess, it didn't work out.
> —Yolanda

After this second attempt, Yolanda stopped trying and, as she put it, "wasted 5 years" of her life on the streets. She and many others whose personal issues overwhelmed them believed that maturation, above all else, eventually helped them cope with their problems and understand the importance of education.

A related theme regarding unsuccessful returns to school was the continued mismatch between an individual participant's academic needs and the ability of the new educational setting to meet those needs. Frequently, these students moved from one traditional school to another, where they experienced the same learning conditions that had contributed to their departure in the first place: large classes, alienation from teachers, unaddressed learning issues, and unengaging curriculum and instructional practices.

Re-enrollment in an alternative setting did not necessarily lead to success, either, as both Yolanda's experience with an alternative GED-based program and Callie's with an online school illustrate. These kinds of less structured, individually paced programs often are touted as an effective alternative for young people who have not done well in a traditional setting. However, the students most likely to succeed in independent, online settings are highly motivated, confident learners (like Jack), not academically struggling discouraged learners (Barbour & Reeves, 2009).

Successful Returns

We considered post-dropout re-enrollments to be "successful" if participants expressed satisfaction with the new setting and viewed themselves as back on a pathway leading to graduation. Participants who defined themselves as successfully re-enrolled tended to be younger at the time of their interview, had not spent time living in foster care or on their own, and had not been involved in criminal activities, according to their accounts. Additional themes connected with a successful return after dropping out included the timing of the re-enrollment, the encouragement and guidance participants received prior to re-enrolling, and the educational and relational characteristics of the new setting.

Support for a Quick Return. A subset of participants spent only a short time (1 or 2 months) out of school before attempting a return, typically at the urging of a parent, counselor, or teacher who helped them navigate their next steps. Having a caring adult advocating and guiding them appeared to be a key element in the quick and relatively successful returns of participants like Xavier, who had maintained a strong connection to a former teacher who stepped in to help:

> My teacher, Mr. Hansen, wanted me to get my credits. . . . He pretty much forced me—to talk to my counselor. . . . And then, he helped me write my essay to get into a credit retrieval program at the alternative school, and now I'm here. He stuck with me all the way through.
> —Xavier

Finding a Better Fit. When the return was to an alternative setting that better fit their needs, the students' truancy abated, while newfound academic successes helped them begin to feel capable and hopeful again. The new learning environments offered some of the positive features they recalled from elementary school: caring personal relationships with teachers, greater choice and control over their learning, and more individualized academic support. For example, for Callie, who had experienced turmoil and conflict at home, the positive personal relationships she found at a new school were key to her engagement:

> That more personal experience, being able to be closer with the teachers and have more one-on-one was what I needed for high

school. I developed a relationship with all three of the teachers I had
. . . the school really was a family, and it's like that's what I needed.
—Callie

Derrick, after a couple of months and with lots of prodding from
parents and a former school counselor, re-enrolled in a small alternative
school in his suburban district, which provided both the connection to
teachers and the more individualized support he craved:

> At this school, all the teachers are committed and help out and that's
> what I like. Like Mr. Hamilton, our math teacher, he always finds time
> for everyone in the class to help them out a little bit. And if you need
> the extra help, he'll, like, sit there and tell everyone to hold on while he
> helps the one person, like, catch them up a little bit . . . and I really like
> that about him. —Derrick

REGRETTING DROPPING OUT

Regardless of the pathways youth participants followed, most expressed
regrets that they had ignored their parents' advice and they bemoaned
their poor decisions about school—decisions that they now saw as big
mistakes. They had discovered that without a high school diploma they
could not readily obtain good jobs, easily live on their own, or fully en-
ter an adult life. Most were now back in an alternative program trying
to recoup credits to graduate (36%) or gain a GED certificate (about
50%). Only a few, like Jack (as described in his full narrative), possessed
the academic skills and confidence necessary to make up for lost time
and aspire to further education. We end this section with some wistful
reflections about dropping out:

> I was too distracted to study or learn. I feel like that's mostly the reason
> why I didn't really have an interest in school and stopped trying. If I
> could go back now, I would do things differently. —Trisha

> If I think about it now, this year would have been my last year and I
> would be graduating by now. But I didn't think about it then, and I
> skipped all the time. —Derrick

> I was really disappointed that I didn't graduate. There wasn't somebody
> who had my back going, "You're doing good." . . . But there was
> nobody really that I could turn to. —Callie

CONCLUSION

The stories of youth participants illustrate the surprising complexity and variation the final act of leaving school can entail. To begin with, determining who actually has dropped out is not always clear-cut; it may make more sense to think of students as being on a truancy–dropout continuum. Some participants moved back and forth on this continuum, attending and then not attending for varying periods of time.

Many students attempted to re-enroll in a high school program, only to drop out again. This cycle of repeated dropping in, dropping out served to further discourage youth participants, most of whom subsequently gave up on graduation (and ultimately turned to a GED program). For some, the fit of the new school setting was problematic; those returning to a traditionally structured or online alternative typically did not last in these settings. This willingness of dropouts to try again presents school districts with an opportunity to re-engage. However, re-engagement is likely to be more successful when students have a strong advocate within the system, guiding them to new settings that offer positive relationships, individual supports, and opportunities for success.

In reflecting on their decision to leave, participants identified a variety of "tipping points" that they believed were significant catalysts to dropping out. Ideally, a dropout prevention effort would identify engagement problems in individual students and intervene well before the student reaches a tipping point. For such efforts to be effective, an awareness of common tipping points is essential; despite a school's best efforts, some students will arrive at such points. Certain school-based events (like bullying or suspension) or personal experiences (such as becoming pregnant or homeless) may function as tipping points, accelerating a student's exit and signaling the need for intervention. Effective dropout prevention must include strategies for reducing such events, as well as mitigating their impacts after they occur. In the final chapter we focus both on schoolwide approaches and on more individualized, classroom-based strategies aimed at preventing students from reaching a tipping point.

CHAPTER 7

Implications and Possibilities

I love the idea of having you talk to people that have dropped out because everyone's got their different stories . . . I think that doing this is gonna help somebody else to graduate. So I really love this idea. —Callie

If we really listened to youth voices, what would we do? In this chapter, we address plausible responses to the themes and issues that emerge from young people's narratives about dropping out. We stress that there is no magic solution or quick fix; indeed, the six youths' narratives featured here illustrate the complex nature of problems and issues that lead to dropping out. To address these issues comprehensively, changes would need to be made at the classroom, school, and district levels; in the very best-case scenario, changes also would be addressed at the macro level to rectify economic and racial inequities that also play a role. Our analysis, however, suggests three principles that could be enacted by educators to mitigate many of the pressing concerns that youths raised:

1. Understand the story behind the behavior
2. Build a caring school community and foster a sense of belonging among students
3. Institute instructional approaches that support and engage struggling students

This final chapter discusses the nature of each principle, offers examples of ways these principles can be enacted, and provides rationales for why these would be effective solutions. These are, in effect, calls to action for teachers, school and district personnel, and policymakers. We end with a consideration of the ways these principles interact and a reflection on larger societal issues and how they impact schooling.

PRINCIPLE 1: UNDERSTAND THE STORY BEHIND THE BEHAVIOR

This first principle captures the need to look carefully at the reasons behind the actions of struggling students. By inquiring into the backstory for why an adolescent has behaved in a certain way, those who work with young people demonstrate caring and the intention to understand and help. Once educators gain insight into the reasons for an individual student's behavior, they can develop informed options for how to reach out to and support the student. Inquiring into the backstory plays an important role in addressing academic as well as behavioral issues.

Discover the Story Behind Problem Behaviors

We have seen over and over again with the six youth participants that issues behind problem behaviors like arguing, getting into fights, and skipping school were often complex, and that school factors played a significant role. When educators do not know the backstory, it is easy to make assumptions or attributions about the student that not only may be incorrect (e.g., the student does not care about school), but also may chip away at the student's commitment to school. These false attributions can lead to feelings of unfair treatment and to unproductive teacher and school responses that exacerbate rather than mitigate the problem. For example, the school disenrolled Xavier, without his knowledge, after a string of unexcused absences when both family and medical issues dominated his life. According to him, the school simply had assumed he was truant and had not bothered to learn more; the school's unilateral move colored his attitude toward the institution from that point on.

Jack's and Trisha's stories of being mercilessly bullied prior to being suspended for fights further illustrate the importance of the backstory. Both these students perceived school personnel to be uninterested in their backstories and incapable of providing a safe learning environment. By enforcing mandatory suspensions for fighting without showing any flexibility or attention to the context or details of the fight, school personnel further alienated already struggling students. If administrators had truly listened, they might have learned more about these students' personal challenges and been better positioned to problem-solve and offer support.

How do youths benefit when adults inquire into the story behind their behavior? First, the very act of inquiring and listening demonstrates caring and respect, serving to build or strengthen a productive relationship between teacher (or administrator or counselor) and student. In addition, a listen-first approach encourages youths to find meaning in their actions, helping them to make sense of their social world and enlarge their reflective capacities to jointly problem-solve and resolve issues (Zemelman, 2016). Finally, the adult in the situation learns valuable information that will help guide interactions with the student and family, thus increasing the adult's sense of efficacy and agency (Hopkins, 2004).

There are many steps that schools can take to help staff find the story behind the behavior; here are two examples.

Provide Professional Development on the Nature of Trauma. Understanding the nature of trauma and adverse childhood experiences (Dube et al., 2001) can help teachers and administrators understand that behavior tells a story and spark their curiosity about what underlies behavior. Professional development could include learning about the effects of trauma on the brain and about trauma-informed practices, such as using breathing exercises and having a safe space in the classroom where a student can choose to go until he has calmed down. In addition, teachers can learn strategies for teaching how emotions affect the brain and what students can do to calm themselves. A focus on social and emotional learning, in addition to academics, can help all students, but especially vulnerable students, learn to self-regulate, develop a sense of agency, and get along better with peers. From a teacher's perspective, using trauma-informed practices also helps with the secondary trauma that teachers often experience when working with vulnerable youth (Perry, 2014).

Adopt Discipline Programs Congruent with Learning the Backstory. Schools and districts can adopt discipline programs such as Restorative Justice or RULER (Hagelskamp Brackett, Rivers, & Salovey, 2013; Hopkins, 2004), which emphasize similar ideas about listening to youths, understanding the story behind their behavior, and helping students to self-regulate and cope better. The 2016 film *Paper Tigers* documents the extraordinary success of Lincoln High School, an alternative school for youth with a history of truancy, substance abuse, and trauma. The sources of this success included teaching the entire staff about adverse childhood experiences and abandoning punitive practices in favor of trauma-informed ones. This approach yielded a dramatic decline in suspensions and expulsions, 75% fewer fights, a substantially increased graduation rate, and three times as many college-bound graduates (Redford & Pritzker, 2016). As this example demonstrates, to help vulnerable students, a discipline program should not merely punish; it also must recognize the effects of trauma on behavior, discover the reasons for misbehavior, and help students become more responsible and accountable for their actions.

Explore Struggling Students' Perspectives to Inform Instructional Choices

Untangling all the factors contributing to poor academic performance is a challenge for educators. Even the youths we interviewed had difficulty distinguishing which of their challenges were due to study habits, mindsets, lack of basic skills, or the nature of the instruction they received. Sometimes school personnel are quick to assume students are doing poorly primarily because they are demonstrably not putting in the effort—not paying attention, not turning in assignments, or missing class. However, backstories from our participants make it clear that a variety of learning issues often precipitate withdrawal of effort. When a teacher asks struggling students key questions about their learning experiences, their answers can shed valuable light on possible causes of poor academic performance. Are they missing an essential concept or study skill that has stymied progress? Have they been unproductive in attempts to complete required work? Have they developed an "I'm no good in math" mindset? Below are some examples of how teachers can use student perspectives to inform instructional practices.

Identify and Address Common Misconceptions That Result in Learning Roadblocks. There is a long tradition in cognitive psychology of exploring common misconceptions that underlie students' errors, especially in science and math (Bransford, Brown, & Cocking, 2000). Such misconceptions undoubtedly played a role in participants' widely reported math woes. Even years later when being interviewed, participants readily summoned up unpleasant memories of being lost in math class. Basic algebraic concepts, like the use of letters to represent unknown values, confused and dismayed many, impeding the progress even of students with no previous learning issues, like Callie and Xavier. When participants' confusions went unaddressed, they quickly snowballed, leading ultimately to an "I'm no good in math" mindset and a withdrawal of effort.

Awareness of common student thinking errors is an essential component of a teacher's pedagogical toolkit in any discipline, but especially in math, which more than any other subject academically upended participants. By being on the lookout for common misconceptions and routinely asking students about their reasoning, teachers can uncover conceptual gaps and errors that hold students back. This approach (an essential departure from the "I-do-you-do" instruction described in Chapter 4) also creates possibilities for flexible, temporary grouping of students, as described later.

Interpret Student Mindsets. Students who have determined that they are not good at a subject often feel helpless and hopeless in the face of learning challenges. If teachers can identify students' negative mindsets, such as "I'm no good at math!," they have an avenue for disrupting those mindsets and developing alternative ones that foster learning (Johnston, 2012). One powerful way of addressing a negative mindset is to remind students that challenge and failure are part of learning: *"I see many of you are having difficulties solving linear equations at the moment; it's not that you aren't good at this, it's that you are not good* yet. *Let's see if we can try using another strategy here."*

Understand Students' Experiences of School

Exploring students' experiences of school can yield important information about unseen barriers to engagement and academic achievement. Indeed, it is the premise of this book that listening to young people helps us understand more deeply the dynamics that lead to their dropping out. Teachers, administrators, and counselors can all benefit from an exploration of students' worlds, gaining valuable insight into their experiences and behavior. Moreover, as Drolet and Arcand (2013) point out, students who otherwise might be wary of authority come to see those who are genuinely inquiring into their school experiences as trustworthy and legitimate. Two noteworthy strategies for accessing student experiences of school are student interviews and shadowing students.

Conduct Short, Focused Interviews. Periodically implementing short, focused interviews that ask students about their experiences and perceptions of school is an excellent way to learn about student perspectives (Drolet & Arcand, 2013; Farrington, 2014). An open-ended interview process potentially deepens relationships between students and the adults conducting the interviews, gives students a forum in which to be heard, and fosters their metacognitive and reflective capacities. Interviews might focus on topics such as bullying, what makes school boring or interesting for students, or the use of new instructional and assessment strategies (e.g., the use of learning targets). Interview results can be shared in faculty meetings, used to make changes, and tracked to gauge the effect of those changes. Students' sense of self-efficacy could be increased if meaningful changes result from their input.

Shadow Students. The practice of shadowing students is an excellent technique for acquiring insight into how students experience school (Ginsberg, 2012). Shadowing can take the form of following and observing one student throughout the school day or actually participating and doing all required work in that student's classes for a day. Educators who engage in this practice say they sometimes are shocked by what a school day looks and feels like from the student's perspective. By shadowing struggling students, teachers, administrators, and counselors may gather clues about what is or is not helping a particular student succeed, how they might better intervene for that student, or what general changes to school and classroom structures might improve students' school experiences.

PRINCIPLE 2:
BUILD A CARING COMMUNITY AND FOSTER
A SENSE OF BELONGING

This second principle concerns the imperative to develop strong relationships with students, create caring communities within the school and in each classroom, and help all youths feel like they belong. As participants' narratives attest, the issue of whether they felt cared for by teachers and other staff made an immense difference in how they experienced school.

Building a caring community goes a long way toward fostering a sense of belonging, diminishing bullying, and setting the stage for learning. Unlike a culture of control, a caring community rests on a foundation of trusting relationships between students and their teachers, or, as Noddings (2005) has termed it, an "ethic of care." Nieto and Bode (2012) assert that solidarity with and empathy for students is one critical aspect of caring that is particularly relevant to helping disengaged students. In elaborating, they point to genuine respect, high expectations, and great admiration for students, as well as *remembering what it was like to be an adolescent.*

Foster Personal Connections Inside the Classroom

Participants celebrated the warm connections they experienced with their teachers through much of elementary school and decried the loss of these connections when they entered secondary school. Those relations were pivotal, as they helped struggling students feel like they belonged, enhanced their enjoyment of school, encouraged them to persevere, and supported them through rough personal times. Once those relational supports disappeared, many struggling students felt abandoned. Some, like Trisha, were unable to ask for help when they desperately needed assistance, and they languished. Others, like Derrick and Xavier, became caught up in a cycle of frustration, anger, and conflict with teachers and other authority figures at school.

While we acknowledge constraints teachers face in many secondary schools, such as large classroom sizes, short instructional time periods, and an ever-changing population of students, teachers can seize opportunities to forge stronger teacher-to-student and peer-to-peer connections. Here are several ideas.

Model and Use Supportive Language. Acknowledging student perspectives with supportive rather than critical language goes a long way toward fostering personal connections. We know from youth narratives, as well as from research on adolescent development, how sensitive teenagers are to facial expressions and tone of voice (Yurgelun-Todd, 2007). Adolescents, especially vulnerable ones, despise sarcasm from teachers (even though students themselves are often masters of the form!) and are quick to interpret teachers' remarks as negative. Derrick, for example, believed teachers were criticizing him when they responded to his questions with phrases like, "We went over that in class." Responses like that failed to recognize Derrick's deep learning issues and increasingly negative mindset about his abilities. Supportive language in this kind of situation might include acknowledging difficulties: *"I see that this problem is especially hard for you; let's see what you were able to do and where you got stuck."* Another important facet of supportive language is to acknowledge learning difficulties while conveying that students are not alone: *"Yes, I'm expecting that many of you will struggle with these challenging problems. But we'll take this slowly, and over time this will get easier for you. I'm here to support you."*

Confer with Individual Students. Reconfiguring instructional time can provide opportunities to know students better. One exemplar is the Reader's Workshop model (Harvey & Goudvis, 2007). This model entails a short mini-lesson to demonstrate a useful strategy, skill, or concept, followed by a block of time for students to immediately practice what they learned in the mini-lesson. During this practice block, while students work independently, the teacher is free to confer with individuals. Conferring provides the space to get to know one's students well; it builds rapport, affords students the opportunity to feel acknowledged, and offers help when needed without public embarrassment. Teachers can use conferring to figure out why students get stuck, explore mindsets, and offer timely strategies to get "unstuck." Cris Tovani (2011) describes how she uses this model to connect with and help struggling readers across different subject areas. Imagine if Trisha's and Derrick's teachers had conferred with them on a regular basis, using a simple, "How is it going?" query to get to know them better and to provide specific strategies for helping them understand assigned readings. Conferring is one potent way to help students feel that they are seen and cared for.

Offer Opportunities for Peer Collaboration. According to youth participants, peer interaction occurred frequently in elementary school through recess, field trips, and other less structured learning activities. However, peer-to-peer learning experiences were remarkably absent from their recollections of middle and high school, despite the potential contribution of peer interaction to school engagement (Pianta & Allen, 2008). Collaborating with peers allows students to get to know one another better and expand their social circles. For socially vulnerable youths (including, as described in Chapter 4, transfer students), positive classroom interactions may decrease their sense of isolation and help keep them engaged in school. However, it is crucial that students learn how to work together effectively (Harvey & Daniels, 2015); teachers can scaffold by explicitly teaching important collaboration skills such as turn-taking and managing disagreements. Collaborative and intentional group work is a distinctly different enterprise than simply telling a student who doesn't understand to get help from a peer. Callie and many other interviewed youths decried this teacher response to their questions and instead withdrew further. In contrast, when group work is open-ended, intellectually stimulating, and requires distinct roles (e.g., note-keeper, visual artist, etc.), collaboration builds social connections and skills while fostering academic engagement.

Embrace Practices That Enhance a Climate of Caring and Connection

Embracing schoolwide structures and practices that foster caring and connection sets a positive tone for staff and students, providing rituals and routines that help to create a safe environment for vulnerable adolescents that promotes positive development in the face of challenges. It is important to note that the school's discipline program plays a critical role in establishing a school climate of caring and connection (Hopkins, 2004). Programs such as Restorative Justice, described under the first principle, foster connection-making and help students feel cared for and understood, while still holding them accountable. Below we provide three additional strategies supportive of developing a caring community.

Conduct Climate Surveys. Periodic "climate surveys" of students, parents, and staff help schools measure stakeholder perceptions regarding the school's safety, inclusiveness, welcoming atmosphere, and other aspects of a caring community. The 2016 federal Every Student Succeeds Act (ESSA) has recognized the importance of school climate, allowing states to choose climate as an indicator of school quality and student success. To support schools' efforts in this area, the Department of Education has funded a series of related online resources, including downloadable surveys, so schools can systematically track how they are doing in this important area and use survey data to make productive changes (National Center on Safe Supportive Learning Environments, 2016).

Institute Advisories. In an advisory period, teachers work to build a caring community through small-group activities and conversations with individual advisees. Advisors use this meeting time to track how each student is doing, enabling a timely intervention as soon as there is a drop-off in attendance or grades. Advisories require significant organizational preparation, including adequate training and support for staff taking on this new role. However, when done well, they foster good peer and student–teacher relations, thus supporting a sense of belonging, especially for students making the transition into middle or high school (Anfara, 2006).

Develop Peer-Mentoring Opportunities. When transitioning (or transferring) to a new school, many youth participants were overwhelmed, both socially and academically. Peer mentoring, used at both the middle and high school levels, is a promising approach for supporting new students and improving short- and long-term outcomes for all students, including those academically at risk (Johnson, Simon, & Mun, 2014). In effective mentoring programs, older students receive substantial training, learning how to serve as advisors and to conduct meetings with their mentees, either in groups or one-on-one. Student mentors benefit from participation in a mentoring program by increasing their communication skills and sense of belonging in school. In addition, peer mentorship programs provide a worthy rite of passage for first-year students or transfers to aspire to when they reach the upper grades; they also give students a way to see how to use their own experiences to benefit others. Multiple resources on peer mentoring are available from the Center for Supportive Schools (www.supportiveschools.org).

Forge Partnerships to Address Nonacademic Needs

Our youth participants faced a host of personal and family issues—issues that required assistance well outside the purview of what teachers and even counselors could offer and that negatively affected their school performance. Students at risk for dropping out may require mental health counseling, drug counseling, family interventions, or help with basic necessities like food and shelter. It is almost impossible for students to concentrate on academics and manage their emotions when they are in crisis, not feeling safe, or not getting basic needs met. The following suggestions may help in addressing these needs.

Consider a Range of School–Community Partnerships. Most communities have a number of organizations that would be willing to partner with schools. Learning about these organizations and what they can offer students in need is an important first step. A more far-reaching idea is to develop a community school model. This model is expressly designed to address the ongoing needs of vulnerable students through structured partnerships with local agencies and foundations.[1] Alternatively, high schools could broaden their scope by including mental and physical health clinics right on campus, as the Walla Walla high school featured in *Paper Tigers* does.

Develop Family–School Partnerships and Conduct Home Visits. When families (whatever form they take) are involved with school, especially at the high school level, students tend to perform better (Henderson & Mapp, 2002). Teachers, counselors, and administrators can foster family–school connections through occasional phone calls home (especially when the call reports on something positive a student has done), regularly scheduled conferences, and exhibitions of student work and other kinds of student presentations. Conducting home visits helps educators to better understand students' home environments and cultural backgrounds and to gain appreciation for what is going on in their lives (Henderson & Mapp, 2002). Learning more about students' lives usually results in an increase in empathy on the part of teachers and a sense of being known (and cared for) on the part of students. Home visits are often helpful in interpreting student behavior and are an important tool of culturally responsive pedagogy (Ladson-Billings, 2014).

PRINCIPLE 3: INSTITUTE INSTRUCTIONAL
APPROACHES THAT SUPPORT AND ENGAGE

Like Derrick and Trisha, many participants had learning needs that were not fully attended to; these needs became particularly compromising in middle and high school, playing a central role in students' disengagement from school. Another theme to emerge from the narratives was that traditional instructional methods and practices often seemed to increase difficulties for struggling students. In this final principle, we address several strategies to honor and work with all young people.

Develop Engaging Curriculum and Instruction

A common refrain throughout all the youth narratives was how boring and irrelevant students found much of their secondary coursework. When asked what might have made a difference in middle and high school, Callie and others responded that they enjoyed projects and appreciated choice; they spoke longingly about their wishes for authentic and relevant learning experiences. Learning in active ways through simulations, fieldwork, role-plays, mock trials, and projects is engaging and rewarding, especially for disaffected youth (Wilhelm, 2002). Experiential modes of learning offer relevant, compelling, and challenging curriculum and support motivation to learn (P. J. Finn, 2009)—all significant aspects of engagement. Below are two ideas to support adolescent engagement in learning.

Include Multiple Opportunities for Student Choice. Youth participants' narratives were remarkable for their scarcity of recollections of engaging activities involving choice. One notable exception is Callie's history project, described in Chapter 4. She waxed enthusiastic over her creative choices, how much she learned, and how engaged she felt. She surprised herself, although researchers would not be surprised (Strobel & van Barneveld, 2009). Student choice could involve selecting from an array of assignments or projects, assessing the level of difficulty of math problems to tackle, or determining which texts they want to read or feel comfortable reading. More ambitious avenues for choice might include having students decide on topics for a Socratic

Seminar, a play to put on (or write), a scientific study to engage in, or a social justice action that would benefit the school or community. Student choice, whether small- or large-scale, accrues benefits for student autonomy and self-efficacy and can enhance collaboration and classroom culture (Ivey & Johnston, 2013).

Connect Curriculum Content to Students' Lives. Curriculum that connects to students' lives imparts a sense of relevance and purpose that may spark engagement (Zemelman, 2016). A unit on immigration, for example, could start with students tracing their own family's immigration or migration stories. Another strategy would be to create place-based curriculum that revolves around problems and issues in the community, requires authentic inquiry, and involves students in generating possible solutions. Examples include examining local water quality for a science class, or interviewing community members on their ideas for sustainable growth for their town. As is obvious from these examples, this type of curriculum also has the virtue of being culturally responsive (Ladson-Billings, 2014) and involving students in the community.

Another way to connect to students' lives is through issues of social justice; these topics often arouse emotion and imbue academic work with purpose, relevance, and urgency. Examples include taking on housing and homeless issues, disproportionate school funding, the placement of polluting factories, and the prevalence of type 2 diabetes across different areas of the city or town. These topics capture the interests—and indignation—of adolescents, while fostering civic engagement (Zemelman, 2016).

Similarly, combining service learning opportunities with coursework makes learning relevant, connects students to people and institutions, and, best of all, helps young people feel that they are of use (Zemelman, 2016). Projects could range from cleaning up riparian zones for a science class to tutoring younger children in reading and writing for an English class. These kinds of learning opportunities help forge new and beneficial relationships with adults in ways that may provide extra support and encouragement for vulnerable students.

Use Supportive Assignment and Grading Practices

The stories from youth participants made it abundantly clear that certain traditional approaches to assignments and grading demotivated struggling students. Imagine how differently students like Derrick, Xavier, and Trisha might have experienced school if their learning issues were acknowledged and dealt with through appropriately calibrated assignments, if their partial learning counted in grades, and if they were given chances to relearn, revise, and redeem (Darling-Hammond, Ramos-Beban, Altamirano, & Hyler, 2016). For starters, these students would have felt attended to and would have experienced the sense of efficacy that comes from mastering a skill or concept that initially was difficult. Their teachers, too, would have experienced the agency that comes from seeing progress. Below we give some examples of supportive practices.

Group Flexibly and Progressively. Flexible and progressive student grouping (i.e., short term, with regrouping as soon as progress is made) allows students time to catch up on missed skills or partially understood concepts, and gives them the help they need when they need it. This kind of grouping is particularly helpful for math and English classes, but also could be used in science or language classes. To be clear, we are not talking about permanent tracking and labeling, which have proven to be detrimental to low-skills students (Farrington, 2014); rather, this is a precise, short-term targeting of instruction matched to learning needs.

For larger secondary schools that offer a number of the same classes at the same time, there are opportunities to immediately address common conceptual issues (described under Principle 1) across a subject area before they become irreversible stumbling blocks. For example, if all pre-algebra teachers gave an ungraded diagnostic test, they then could temporarily rearrange classes to have one teacher work with the students who needed more help mastering a particular concept while other teachers worked with those ready to move on. Such an approach might have allowed Callie, Derrick, and the many others who struggled in middle school math classes to receive more individualized, targeted assistance in a timely way.

Restructure Grading Practices to Motivate and Support Learning. Academically, there is nothing more disheartening than a failing grade. Youth participants who repeatedly received failing grades internalized them as a judgment on their abilities, even when the low grades resulted from skipping class or not turning in work. Grading homework assignments can be particularly counterproductive, especially if missed assignments result in an automatic zero. As Norrell (2015) has noted, "Handing out zeros for missed assignments boils down to a disciplinary measure, one that prevents schools from effectively assessing their students' learning." Instead of grading homework, treating it as a source of formative assessment and evidence of progress toward learning targets may motivate students to do their homework.

A similar argument for change can be made concerning test grades. When a student receives a 50 (out of a 100) on a test, she knows only that she has flunked; she does not recognize that she actually has mastered half of the material. What if, instead, tests were analyzed in terms of the learning targets or objectives they were designed to measure? Students then could examine which learning targets they had mastered and which they still needed to work on. Taking the approach a step further, what if students then were given time to work on the targets they hadn't yet mastered and were able to retake that portion of the test? In these ways, the assessment system could be focused on continual learning, not on grading and sorting, with the added benefit of promoting a growth mindset: "I haven't achieved these learning targets *yet.*"

Use Proficiency-Based Grading to Evaluate Learning. Some schools are abandoning grades altogether and using different approaches that help students to evaluate and reflect on their own learning. For example, schools are replacing tests with performance-based assessments and portfolio presentations—assessment practices that align well with the projects and experiential learning described earlier (McTighe & O'Connor, 2005). Alternatives to testing can spark greater student interest and motivation because these approaches build in an audience, tap creativity and choice, and allow time to revise and succeed. Finally, some school districts are replacing traditional letter grades with proficiency-based grading, an approach that can help struggling students see more clearly what they have achieved so far and what they still need to work on (O'Connor, 2009). This promotes learning while removing the punitive sting of a letter grade.

Reduce or Eliminate Homework. The value of homework is up for debate. For many of the interviewed youth, homework constituted one more alienating learning experience. Many did not sufficiently understand their assignments and did not have someone at home to turn to for help. Some were homeless or, like Callie, faced other challenging living situations that made completing homework difficult, if not impossible. Prominent educational thinkers assert that homework is of little benefit to learning: They cite the lack of empirical evidence supporting the practice and observe that homework often consists of rote exercises or assignments that are not differentiated enough to be of use to every student in a class (Harvey & Daniels, 2015). Thus, homework feels like a waste of time for students who already understand the material or is simply another demotivating experience for students who do not. If teachers must assign homework, they should avoid selecting undifferentiated homework assignments that can inadvertently subvert the learning enterprise.

Work Proactively with Struggling Students

Almost all our participants faced learning challenges that set the stage for disengagement and dropping out. Their learning struggles compounded over time: What was manageable in elementary school became insurmountable in high school. From their narratives it is clear that learning issues become emotional issues affecting academic mindsets and identities, often leading to an "I'm a loser" mentality. The important idea here is that learning issues need to be diagnosed and attended to as soon as possible; students with learning gaps need to be given not only adequate support but also sufficient time to catch up.

Access to useful and immediate help is both an equity and instructional issue. In middle- and upper-income families, if a child is struggling, parents either work with the child or they pay someone with expertise to do so, an option not financially viable for lower-income families. For the sake of equity, schools need to take on this tutoring role with students who do not have access to help from their families. If schools do not proactively attend to learning issues, students are doomed to unsuccessful school careers, and their academic identities as failures are sealed. How might schools work with students where this kind of familial help is not available? Below are some concrete suggestions, most of which could be implemented without huge changes in structure or time commitments.

Assess to Identify Strengths and Progress. An important first step is to carefully assess students' current academic strengths and areas in which they are in need of support. A diagnostic test at the beginning of the year can help teachers identify stumbling blocks that might get in the way of student growth in math, for example. In addition, students benefit from ongoing assessment geared toward identifying progress made toward achieving learning targets. When students see some evidence of progress, it may well disrupt fixed mindsets. Teachers can help struggling students persevere, develop stamina, and shore up academic identities when they point out and name students' progress and strengths and suggest ways students might capitalize on those strengths.

Proactively Check in with Struggling Students. We have seen that, for a variety of reasons, struggling students often become wary of teachers and hesitant to ask for help. Teachers should not wait for students to approach them with questions or concerns. If a struggling student is getting assignment information or help from a classmate, teachers ideally should circle back to that student to check for understanding. At the same time, teachers should look for opportunities to encourage and reward help-seeking behavior, so that reluctant students develop this important academic strategy. Finally, if teachers express concern when students miss classes or assignments, it lets the students know that the teacher is paying attention and that their absences were noticed. These relatively simple and straightforward actions do much to make students feel cared for and supported so that they are less likely to be overwhelmed by new challenges.

Develop a Systemwide Approach to Identifying and Aiding Struggling Students. We know that a sizable percentage of the youths we interviewed faced various learning challenges in elementary school or described themselves as academically unprepared for work in middle and high school, especially in math. While most were able to persevere through middle school, a portion never made it to 9th grade. To adequately address lack of academic preparation and learning challenges requires system-level changes: The entire school system needs to develop an integrated approach to identifying and supporting struggling students across the K–12 (or, ideally, the pre-K–14) continuum. In other words, the goal of raising graduation rates must be a shared, systemwide goal. Early warning systems, for example, need to be deployed starting in elementary school, and these systems should not only focus on predictive indicators of risk (like grades and absences), but also promptly identify and address individual academic and behavioral needs. Moreover, specific, detailed communication about academically struggling students must occur as they transition from elementary to middle school and from middle to high school; plans should be in place to help mitigate difficulties as soon as students transition into a new school.

CONCLUSION

It is evident that the principles and calls to action discussed above are intertwined; taking up one thread inevitably tugs other threads. If educators focus on developing caring relationships, they bolster students' sense of belonging; if teachers commit to creating compelling curriculum, they engage and motivate students; if instructional practices allow room for conferring and group work, teachers come to know their students better and students get to know one another better, which, in turn, enhances a sense of belonging and fosters the positive noncognitive factors that lead to academic success. If educators involve students in formative assessment and use ongoing assessment to immediately inform instruction and articulate helpful feedback, students feel empowered to take the next steps and more hopeful about the outcome. These interconnections form a virtuous cycle that will help keep youth off the pathway to dropping out. Educators can begin to implement many aspects of these principles immediately, while making inroads on the more systemic and structural elements in need of change.

The principles and calls to action discussed above are excellent measures that exist within the locus of control of school districts, schools, teachers, and counselors. However, it is also important to note that there are out-of-school factors and equity issues that demand a societal and governmental response, including poverty, health care, employment opportunities, transportation, housing, and drug rehabilitation. The relationship between these societal issues and school success or failure is well documented (Milner, 2015), informing many of the themes that emerged from the youth narratives, even without the youths' conscious awareness. Establishing community schools that provide on-site mental and physical health clinics, and that attend to food and housing needs, would go a long way toward mitigating the struggles many adolescents experience.

Here is a final quote that captures the underlying spirit of the three principles articulated in this chapter:

> When we as teachers recognize that we are partners with our students in life's long and complex journey, when we begin to treat them with the dignity and respect they deserve for simply being, then we are on the road to becoming worthy teachers. It is just that simple—and just that difficult. —William Ayers, p. 37 (2003)

The three principles, along with the more specific calls to action and examples, begin to address how, every day, we can treat all youths with dignity and respect. Treating students with dignity and respect addresses the wishes participants expressed throughout their interviews: to be included, supported academically, honored for their efforts, cared for, and, most important, heard. This chapter started with a quote from Callie about how we might make a difference through listening to struggling students. Let us heed her call.

Notes

Chapter 1

1. For example, several school districts serving lower-income families discovered that an additional 11%–12% of graduating students had scraped by with a grade point average below 2.0. The worry is that the career and life trajectories of these graduates may not be substantially different from those of peers who dropped out (Community Center for Education Results, 2014).

2. The graduation figures are based on the Four-Year Adjusted Cohort Graduation Rate (ACGR), the standard graduation measure used by the Department of Education (defined at nces.ed.gov).

3. The National High School Center (www.betterhighschools.org), for example, has developed and made widely available an early-warning-system tool for middle grades, as well as for high school.

Chapter 2

1. Farrington et al. (2012) draw a distinction between "academic perseverance" and "academic behaviors." For simplicity's sake, we have focused on academic behaviors as the more all-encompassing term. Both academic behaviors and perseverance are deeply connected to mindset, as influences on, as well as outcomes of, mindset.

Chapter 6

1. In the 1993 movie *Groundhog Day*, Bill Murray plays a weatherman who finds himself trapped in time and must relive the same day over and over again.

Chapter 7

1. See www.communitiesinschools.org/our-work/our-unique-model/#step —cis-affiliates

Washington Student Oral Histories Project Study Details

The Washington Student Oral Histories Project was a collaborative effort to collect and analyze the oral histories of young people in western Washington State who had dropped out of school.

Participants

During 2012–2013 we gathered oral histories from a racially, ethnically, and geographically diverse group of 53 youths between the ages of 16 and 22 who previously had dropped out of school. For this study, we considered anyone who self-reported having stayed completely out of school for a total of 1 month or more to have "dropped out." Being truant for a month virtually ensured that students would be too far behind to catch up and would fail their classes for either the semester or the year.

Males constituted 62% of youths interviewed and females 38%, a split that is in keeping with the substantially lower national graduation rates of males (Snyder et al., 2016). Racially and ethnically, the sample was diverse, but not necessarily representative of dropout rates for different groups in the state. African Americans, making up 25% of the sample, were overrepresented, while Hispanics, at 11%, were underrepresented. Native American and Asian youths each constituted 8%, 5% were multiracial or "other," while White youths were 43% of the sample. The sample included participants from urban communities (45%), rural communities (27%), and suburban communities (28%). Although the study did not directly document family economic status, the information youths volunteered about their family struggles and living circumstances indicates that all but a handful likely came from low- or lower-middle-income families.

To promote further diversity in our sample, we deliberately chose recruitment sites that served different populations of dropouts in different kinds of communities. For example, two partnering agencies were alternative schools that served younger youths interested in obtaining a diploma. Most had dropped out of a traditional high school for a relatively short time (less than a year), then re-enrolled in the alternative option. In contrast, three other sites offered multiple services to older teens and young adults. Participants drawn from these sites were usually older and seeking a GED credential. Because we relied on a site-based recruitment model, our interview sample excluded those who had dropped out and remained disconnected from educational services. These youths might differ from those in our interview sample in unknown ways.

Interviews

To ensure candid and safe conversations, we interviewed young people individually at five organizations serving youth who had dropped out. We used a semistructured protocol (Patton, 2002) to guide the interviews. This protocol specified general content areas to be investigated in each interview while also providing flexibility to improvise follow-up questions and clarify meaning through layered exchanges with the interviewee (Kvale & Brinkmann, 2009). The hour-long individual interviews focused particularly on classroom interactions and institutional arrangements that influence a student's engagement, development as a learner, and motivation to stay in school (Eccles et al., 1991; Neild, 2009). Because of their age and potential vulnerability, we purposely did not probe interviewees on sensitive topics such as substance abuse, mental health concerns, family problems, economic status, or criminal history. Nonetheless, the majority of youth volunteered this type of information, allowing us to incorporate it into our analysis.

Narratives

After completing interviews, we used qualitative data analysis software to code and analyze the recorded and transcribed interviews. Our analysis, which allowed us to identify major trends and significant themes across participant interviews, formed the basis of this book. It also informed the selection of six representative youths whose experiences provide examples of our key findings. Utilizing narrative research methodology (Riessman, 1993; Sikes, 2005), we transformed transcripts from these youths' interviews into first-person narratives in order to illustrate trends and themes from their own unique perspectives.

Wherever possible, we use the youths' own words in the narratives. At the same time, we took three steps to protect the identity of these individuals. First, we replaced all names (including place names) with pseudonyms. Second, we altered minor details in order to mask individual identities. For example, in some instances we changed the gender of a family member or teacher who figured prominently in events described by the interviewee. Finally, drawing upon the process of creating composite narratives (Connelly, Clandinin, & He, 1997), we incorporated minor elements of other youth narratives into these six, based on profile and experience similarities, to further protect youth identities without altering core stories or dropping out trajectories.

References

Almasi, J., McKeown, M., & Beck, I. (1996). The nature of engaged reading in classroom discussions of literature. *Journal of Literacy Research, 28*(1), 107–146.

America's Promise Alliance (2014). *Don't call them dropouts: Understanding the experiences of young people who leave high school before graduation.* Washington, DC: Author.

Anfara, Jr., V. A. (2006). *Research summary: Advisory programs.* Westerville, OH: National Middle School Association.

Ayers, W. (2003). The mystery of teaching. In *The Jossey-Bass reader on teaching* (pp. 26–37). New York, NY: Wiley.

Balfanz, R., Herzog, L., & Mac Iver, D. J. (2007). Preventing student disengagement and keeping students on the graduation path in urban middle-grades schools: Early identification and effective interventions. *Educational Psychologist, 42*(4), 223–235.

Bandura, A. (1997). *Self-efficacy: The exercise of control.* New York, NY: Freeman.

Barbour, M. K., & Reeves, T. C. (2009). The reality of virtual schools: A review of the literature. *Computers & Education, 52*(2), 402–416.

Boaler, J. (2015, December). The math-class paradox. *The Atlantic, 316*(5). Retrieved from www.theatlantic.com/education/archive/2015/12/math-class -performing/421710/

Bransford, J. D., Brown, A. L., & Cocking, R. R. (Eds.). (2000). *How people learn: Brain, mind, experience, and school* (exp. ed.). Washington, DC: National Academy Press.

Breslau, J. (2010). *Health in childhood and adolescence and high school dropout* (Report No. 17). Santa Barbara: University of California, Santa Barbara, California Dropout Research Project.

Bridgeland, J. M., Dilulio, J. J., & Morison, K. B. (2006). *The silent epidemic: Perspectives of high school dropouts.* Washington, DC: Civic Enterprises.

Brown, R. (2002). Straddling two worlds: Self-directed comprehension instruction for middle schoolers. In C. C. Block & M. Pressley (Eds.), *Comprehension instruction: Research-based best practices* (pp. 337–350). New York, NY: Guilford Press.

Civic Enterprises & Everyone Graduates Center, Johns Hopkins University School of Education. (2016). *Building a grad nation: Data brief: Overview of 2013-14 high school graduation rates.* Washington, DC: America's Promise Alliance.

Community Center for Education Results. (2014). *The Road Map Project prevalence report*. Retrieved from www.roadmapproject.org/wp-content/uploads/2013/09/Opportunity-Youth-Prevalence.pdf

Connelly, F. M., Clandinin, D. J., & He, M. F. (1997). Teachers' personal practical knowledge on the professional knowledge landscape. *Teaching and Teacher Education, 13*(7), 665–674.

Croninger, R. G., & Lee, V. E. (2001). Social capital and dropping out of high school: Benefits to at-risk students of teachers' support and guidance. *Teachers College Record, 103*(4), 548–581.

Crosnoe, R. (2006). The connection between academic failure and adolescent drinking in secondary school. *Sociology of Education, 79*(1), 44–60.

Darling-Hammond, L., Ramos-Beban, N., Altamirano, R. P., & Hyler, M. E. (2016). *Be the change: Reinventing school for student success*. New York, NY: Teachers College Press.

Day, A. (2011). *An examination of post-secondary education access, retention, and success of foster care youth* (Doctoral dissertation). Western Michigan University, Kalamazoo.

Dijkstra, P., Kuyper, H., van der Werf, G., Buunk, A. P., & van der Zee, Y. G. (2008). Social comparison in the classroom: A review. *Review of Educational Research, 78*(4), 828–879.

Drolet, M., & Arcand, I. (2013). Positive development, sense of belonging, and support of peers among early adolescents: Perspectives of different actors. *International Education Studies, 6*(4), 29–38.

Dube, S. R., Anda, R. F., Felitti, V. J., Chapman, D. P., Williamson, D. F., & Giles, W. H. (2001). Childhood abuse, household dysfunction, and the risk of attempted suicide throughout the life span: Findings from the Adverse Childhood Experiences Study. *JAMA, 286*(24), 3089.

Duckworth, A. (2016). *Grit: The power of passion and perseverance*. New York, NY: Scribner.

Dweck, C. S. (2006). *Mindset: The new psychology of success*. New York, NY: Random House.

Eccles, J. S., Lord, S., & Midgley, C. (1991). What are we doing to early adolescents? The impact of educational contexts on early adolescents. *American Journal of Education, 99*(4), 521–542.

Eccles, J. S., & Roeser, R. W. (2009). Schools, academic motivation, and stage–environment fit. In R. M. Lerner & L. Steinberg (Eds.), *Handbook of adolescent psychology* (3rd ed., Vol. 1, pp. 404–434). Hoboken, NJ: Wiley.

Ehri, L. C. (1995). Phases of development in learning to read words by sight. *Journal of Research in Reading, 18*(2), 116–125.

Ewert, S. (2012). *What it's worth: Field of training and economic status in 2009* (Current Population Reports). Washington, DC: U.S. Census Bureau.

Fabelo, T., Thompson, M., Plotkin, M., Carmichael, D., Marchbanks, M., & Booth, E. (2011). *Breaking schools' rules: A statewide study of how school discipline relates to students' success and juvenile justice involvement*. Austin: Council of State Governments Justice Center & Public Policy Research Institute at Texas A&M University.

Farrington, C. A. (2014). *Failing at school: Lessons for redesigning urban high schools*. New York, NY: Teachers College Press.

Farrington, C. A., Roderick, M., Allensworth, E., Nagaoka, J., Keyes, T. S., Johnson, D. W., & Beechum, N. O. (2012). *Teaching adolescents to become learners: The role of noncognitive factors in shaping school performance: A critical literature review*. Chicago, IL: University of Chicago Consortium on Chicago School Research.

Finn, J. D. (1989). Withdrawing from school. *Review of Educational Research, 59*(2), 117–142.

Finn, P. J. (2009). *Literacy with an attitude: Educating working-class children in their own self-interest* (2nd ed.). Albany: State University of New York Press.

Fredricks, J. A., Blumenfeld, P. C., & Paris, A. H. (2004). School engagement: Potential of the concept, state of the evidence. *Review of Educational Research, 74*(1), 59–109.

Freudenberg, N., & Ruglis, J. (2007). Reframing school dropout as a public health issue. *Preventing Chronic Disease, 4*(4), 1–11.

Ginsberg, M. B. (2012, December). Stepping into a student's shoes. *Educational Leadership, 69*(5). Retrieved from http://www.ascd.org/publications/educational -leadership/feb12/vol69/num05/Stepping-into-a-Student%27s-Shoes.aspx

Guthrie, J. T., Klauda, S. L., & Ho, A. N. (2013). Modeling the relationships among reading instruction, motivation, engagement, and achievement for adolescents. *Reading Research Quarterly, 48*(1), 9–26.

Hagelskamp, C., Brackett, M. A., Rivers, S. E., & Salovey, P. (2013). Improving classroom quality with the RULER approach to social and emotional learning: Proximal and distal outcomes. *American Journal of Community Psychology, 51*(3–4), 530–543.

Harvey, S., & Daniels, H. (2015). *Comprehension & collaboration: Inquiry circles for curiosity, engagement, and understanding* (rev. ed.). Portsmouth, NH: Heinemann.

Harvey, S., & Goudvis, A. (2007). *Strategies that work: Teaching comprehension for understanding and engagement* (2nd ed.). Portland, ME: Stenhouse.

Henderson, A. T., & Mapp, K. L. (2002). *A new wave of evidence: The impact of school, family, and community connections on student achievement* (Annual Synthesis 2002). Austin, TX: National Center for Family & Community Connections with Schools, Southwest Educational Development Laboratory.

Hoeve, M., Dubas, J. S., Eichelsheim, V. I., van der Laan, P. H., Smeenk, W., & Gerris, J.R.M. (2009). The relationship between parenting and delinquency: A meta-analysis. *Journal of Abnormal Child Psychology, 37*(6), 749–775.

Hopkins, B. (2004). *Just schools: A whole school approach to restorative justice*. London, England: J. Kingsley Publishers.

Ivey, G., & Johnston, P. H. (2013). Engagement with young adult literature: Outcomes and processes. *Reading Research Quarterly, 48*(3), 255–275.

Johnson, V. L., Simon, P., & Mun, E.-Y. (2014). A peer-led high school transition program increases graduation rates among Latino males. *The Journal of Educational Research, 107*(3), 186–196.

Johnston, P. H. (2012). *Opening minds: Using language to change lives.* Portland, ME: Stenhouse.

Kamenetz, A., & NPR member stations. (2015, June 12). *The truth about America's graduation rates* (online summary). National Public Radio.

Kitsantas, A., Cheema, J., & Ware, H. W. (2011). Mathematics achievement: The role of homework and self-efficacy beliefs. *Journal of Advanced Academics, 22*(2), 310–339.

Kvale, S., & Brinkmann, S. (2009). *InterViews: Learning the craft of qualitative research interviewing.* Thousand Oaks, CA: Sage.

Ladson-Billings, G. (2014). Culturally relevant pedagogy 2.0: A.k.a. the remix. *Harvard Educational Review, 84*(1), 74–84.

Legal Center for Foster Care & Education. (2014). *Fostering success in education: National factsheet on the educational outcomes of children in foster care.* Washington, DC: American Bar Association, Center on Children and the Law.

Legault, L., Green-Demers, I., & Pelletier, L. (2006). Why do high school students lack motivation in the classroom? Toward an understanding of academic motivation and the role of social support. *Journal of Educational Psychology, 98*(3), 567–582.

Lipsey, M. W., & Derzon, J. H. (1998). Predictors of violent or serious delinquency in adolescence and early adulthood: A synthesis of longitudinal research. In R. Loeber & D. P. Farrington (Eds.), *Serious & violent juvenile offenders: Risk factors and successful interventions* (pp. 86–105). Thousand Oaks, CA: Sage.

McKenna, M. C., Kear, D. J., & Ellsworth, R. A. (1995). Children's attitudes toward reading: A national survey. *Reading Research Quarterly, 30*(4), 934–956.

McKinney, S. (2013). *Truancy: A research brief* (Research Brief Series). New York, NY: Status Offense Reform Center, Vera Institute of Justice.

McTighe, J., & O'Connor, K. (2005). Seven practices for effective learning. *Educational Leadership, 63*(3), 10–17.

Milner, H. R. (2015). *Rac(e)ing to class: Confronting poverty and race in schools and classrooms.* Cambridge, MA: Harvard Education Press.

National Academies of Sciences, Engineering, and Medicine. (2016). *Preventing bullying through science, policy, and practice* (F. Rivara & S. L. Menestrel, Eds.). Washington, DC: National Academies Press.

National Center on Safe Supportive Learning Environments. (2016). ED school climate surveys. Retrieved from safesupportivelearning.ed.gov/edscls/administration

National Mathematics Advisory Panel. (2008). *Foundations for success: The final report of the National Mathematics Advisory Panel.* Washington, DC: U.S. Department of Education.

National Research Council. (2004). *Engaging schools: Fostering high school students' motivation to learn.* Washington, DC: National Academies Press.

Neild, R. (2009). Falling off track during the transition to high school: What we know and what can be done. *Future of Children, 19*(1), 53–76.

Nieto, S., & Bode, P. (2012). *Affirming diversity: The sociopolitical context of multicultural education* (6th ed.). Boston, MA: Pearson/Allyn & Bacon.

Noddings, N. (2005). *The challenge to care in schools: An alternative approach to education* (2nd ed.). New York, NY: Teachers College Press.

Norrell, P. (2015). Less than zero. *American School Board Journal.* Retrieved from www.nsba.org/newsroom/american-school-board-journal/latest-edition/less-zero

O'Connor, K. (2009). *How to grade for learning, K–12* (3rd ed.). Thousand Oaks, CA: Corwin.

Patton, M. Q. (2002). *Qualitative research & evaluation methods* (3rd ed.). Thousand Oaks, CA: Sage.

Perry, B. (2014). *The cost of caring: Secondary traumatic stress and the impact of working with high-risk children and families.* Houston, TX: Child Trauma Academy.

Pianta, R. C., & Allen, J. P. (2008). Building capacity for positive youth development in secondary school classrooms: Changing teachers' interactions with students. In M. Shinn & H. Yoshikawa (Eds.), *Toward positive youth development: Transforming schools and community programs* (pp. 21–39). New York, NY: Oxford University Press.

Pianta, R. C., Hamre, B. K., & Allen, J. P. (2012). Teacher–student relationships and engagement: Conceptualizing, measuring, and improving the capacity of classroom interactions. In S. L. Christenson, A. L. Reschly, & C. Wylie (Eds.), *Handbook of research on student engagement* (pp. 365–386). New York, NY: Springer.

Ramirez, G., Gunderson, E. A., Levine, S. C., & Beilock, S. L. (2013). Math anxiety, working memory, and math achievement in early elementary school. *Journal of Cognition and Development, 14*(2), 187–202.

Redford, J., & Pritzker, K. (2016). Teaching traumatized kids. *The Atlantic.* Retrieved from www.theatlantic.com/education/archive/2016/07/teaching-traumatized-kids/490214/

Rich, M. (2015, December 27). As graduation rates rise, a fear diplomas fall short. *New York Times,* p. A1.

Riessman, C. K. (1993). *Narrative analysis.* Newbury Park, CA: Sage.

Rotermund, S. (2007). *Why students drop out of high school: Comparisons from three national surveys* (Statistical Brief No. 2). Santa Barbara: University of California, Santa Barbara, California Dropout Research Project.

Rumberger, R. W. (2011). *Dropping out: Why students drop out of high school and what can be done about it.* Cambridge, MA: Harvard University Press.

Rumberger, R. W., & Lim, S. A. (2008). *Why students drop out of school: A review of 25 years of research* (Policy Brief). Santa Barbara: University of California, Santa Barbara, California Dropout Research Project.

Sikes, P. (2005). Storying schools: Issues around attempts to create a sense of feel and place in narrative research writing. *Qualitative Research 5*(1), 79–94.

Skiba, R., & Peterson, R. (1999). The dark side of zero tolerance: Can punishment lead to safe schools? *Phi Delta Kappan, 80*(5), 372–376, 381–382.

Snyder, T. D., de Brey, C., & Dillow, S. A. (2016). *Digest of Education Statistics 2014* (NCES 2016-006). Washington, DC: National Center for Education Statistics, Institute of Education Sciences, U.S. Department of Education.

Stetser, M., & Stillwell, R. (2014). *Public high school four-year on-time graduation rates and event dropout rates: School years 2010–11 and 2011–12* (No. 2014-391). Washington, DC: National Center for Education Statistics, Institute of Education Sciences, U.S. Department of Education.

Strobel, J., & van Barneveld, A. (2009). When is PBL more effective? A meta-synthesis of meta-analyses comparing PBL to conventional classrooms. *Interdisciplinary Journal of Problem-Based Learning, 3*(1), 45–58.

Swanson, C. (2009). *Cities in crisis 2009: Closing the graduation gap.* Bethesda, MD: Editorial Projects in Education Research Center.

Taylor, L. (2014). *When do California students drop out of school? An update to statistical brief 9* (Statistical Brief No. 18). Santa Barbara: University of California, Santa Barbara, California Dropout Research Project.

Tough, P. (2016). How kids learn resilience. *The Atlantic, 317*(5), 56–66.

Tovani, C. (2011). *So what do they really know? Assessment that informs teaching and learning.* Portland, ME: Stenhouse.

Turner, C. (2015, June 10). Raising graduation rates with questionable quick fixes. *Morning Edition.* Washington, DC: National Public Radio. Retrieved from www.npr.org/sections/ed/2015/06/10/412240568/raising-graduation-rates-with-questionable-quick-fixes

Tyler, J. H., & Lofstrom, M. (2009). Finishing high school: Alternative pathways and dropout recovery. *The Future of Children, 19*(1), 77–103.

Wilhelm, J. D. (2002). *Action strategies for deepening comprehension: Role plays, text structure tableaux, talking statues, and other enactment techniques that engage students with text.* New York, NY: Scholastic Professional Books.

Yurgelun-Todd, D. (2007). Emotional and cognitive changes during adolescence. *Current Opinion in Neurobiology, 17*(2), 251–257.

Zemelman, S. (2016). *From inquiry to action: Civic engagement with project-based learning in all content areas.* Portsmouth, NH: Heinemann.

Zimmer-Gembeck, M. J., & Collins, W. A. (2003). Autonomy development during adolescence. In G. R. Adams & M. Berzonsky (Eds.), *Blackwell handbook of adolescence* (pp. 175–204). Oxford, UK: Blackwell.

Index

About the Authors

Deborah L. Feldman is a senior research consultant with over 25 years of experience in human services–related research. Since 1993 she has operated her own consulting firm, providing pragmatic evaluation and research services to government and nonprofit organizations. She has led training workshops on planning and managing an evaluation and has served as principal evaluator on numerous federally funded projects. Deborah's research has centered on improving juvenile justice, education, and prevention programs for at-risk youth. Her strong personal interest in examining the dropout issue stems from her extensive work with programs for court-involved youth, a population for whom school problems figure prominently.

Antony T. Smith is an associate professor in the School of Educational Studies at the University of Washington Bothell. A former transitional bilingual educator and classroom teacher in the Seattle area, Antony's current teaching and research focus on literacy curriculum and instruction, disciplinary literacy, and teacher education and professional learning. His research utilizes qualitative case study design and narrative research methodology. Antony loves to read novels, cook, and travel. Recent publications include articles in *Educational Leadership*, *The Reading Teacher*, and *Voices from the Middle*.

Barbara L. Waxman is an adjunct professor at Western Washington University, where she teaches in an innovative alternative-route teacher education program designed to foster a diverse teaching force. A long-time K–12 educational consultant in literacy, assessment, curriculum development, school culture, and leadership coaching, Barbara views all these areas as opportunities to further the cause of equity and social justice. For 12 years, she promoted innovative school reform strategies nationally for Expeditionary Learning Education, where she was associate director for professional development. Barbara also conducts evaluations for education programs. Her current research interests focus on critical literacy, equity pedagogy, and teacher education. She loves to read, garden, and travel.